S0-ADT-721

MANIFEST NOW

IDIL AHMED

MANIFEST NOW

A step-by-step guide with tools, techniques, and proven strategies to raise your frequency and create the reality you want.

Copyright © 2018 by Idil Ahmed

All rights reserved. This book or any portion thereof may not be reproduced or used in any manner whatsoever without the express written permission of the publisher except for the use of brief quotations in a book review.

Cover Art: J Slattum

Printed in the United States of America

First Printing, 2018

ISBN Print 978-1-7323885-0-5

Instagram: Idillionaire

Twitter: Idillionaire

Facebook: Idillionaire

Book Club: Idillionairebookclub

Idil Ahmed
San Diego, CA 92037
www.idillionaire.com

I dedicate this book to all the readers
whose lives are about to change forever.

Table of Contents

Introduction

Congratulations on taking the first step toward changing your life and manifesting your dreams. For the longest time, I have been writing about the power of the mind to help inspire millions all over the world to believe in themselves.

I have finally decided to put all the tools, techniques, wisdom, and insights that have helped me create the life I want into this book, so it can also help you get started on manifesting your dreams. What I am going to share in this book will guide you to remove any limitations, blocks, or beliefs that hinder you from creating the abundance you deserve. When I first discovered that I could create my reality, everything in my life changed. I started to see how my thoughts were influencing my life. I learned that we are either unconsciously creating or actively conscious of everything we create.

There was a time in my life when I was unconsciously creating my reality, and wondering why certain things were happening that I wasn't happy about. Like most people, I thought things were out of my control until I discovered how to guide my mental energy to manifest, create, and materialize exactly what I wanted. Once I decided that I was going to be doing the self-work and investing in myself, I began to notice how powerful I am.

Everything can easily change for you, too. You need to focus and concentrate upon the fact that all is possible. I believe we all have the power to completely transform our lives. You need to have a vision, and believe in that vision so deeply that it has no choice but to show up. This is exactly what I did. I focused, created healthier habits, and learned how to harness my mental energy.

This book is very special to me, because I know the positive impact it will have on you as you also begin to discover your own light and tap into hidden possibilities. You are here to remember your innate, God-given powers and experience the abundance that naturally belongs to you. There is no shortage. There is no lack. Once you realize this, things will instantly change for you, because you will now be aware of what your mind can do. In this book, I will walk you through the mental, physical, and spiritual aspects of manifesting. I'll also teach you how to raise your frequency so you can be aligned with what you want to receive.

What You'll Get in This Book

This book will explain to you everything you need to know on the mental, physical, and spiritual level about manifesting, and teach you how to raise your vibration and align yourself with everything your heart desires. The goal here is to help you remember that you are a natural-born manifestor. Everything you think and feel is constantly attracting your reality.

Throughout this book, you will receive guidance to help shed old patterns that no longer serve you, so you can make room for new energy to enter your life. There will be many *aha* moments when you'll remember your innate truth and natural powers. This book will also help you go deeper, so you can release any mental limitations, blocks, and/or negative self-talk that could be in the way of your dreams and visions. Once you realize what is holding you back, you can begin the transformation process by using the tools, tips, and techniques offered here.

I'll be guiding you to create a healthier mental space, recognize your divine love flow, optimize your physical energy, and tap into your spiritual powers. You will also learn how to let go, surrender, allow, and take action when necessary. What you'll receive here will change how you think, feel, and look at your life. You'll start to understand that you are a powerful, magnetic being with the potential to attract unlimited abundance, happiness, love, and solutions in order to be at peace with yourself, no matter what the circumstances. It's time to reprogram your mind to wealth, beauty, and unlimited resources. There is plenty for everyone to succeed and do what they love. Get ready to manifest your wildest dreams.

Manifest Now starts by guiding you through the mental, physical, and spiritual aspects of manifesting and creating what you want. You'll learn how to start removing mental and emotional blocks so you can rediscover your natural birthright. You'll feel more confident, reconnected, and powerful when you read this book. Everything in your life will start to shift as you begin to realize that you are a conscious creator.

This book also features four sections that will assist you in manifesting your dreams. The first section, "Release It," contains 10 powerful techniques you can use on a daily basis to release any mental, physical, or emotional blocks that hinder your manifesting powers. The second section, "Think It," contains 35 powerful thoughts to keep you energized, focused, and excited to manifest. I offer words to read on a daily basis to keep your frequency high, so you can manifest instantly. The third section, "Affirm It," contains 100 affirmations that will help you start speaking, feeling, and commanding greatness, abundance, happiness, and financial freedom into your life right now. The last section, "Magnetic Money Mindset," focuses on finding your purpose, doing what you love, and attracting financial freedom along the way. This section contains all of my mental hacks, secrets, tips, insights, and wisdom for manifesting money. Also included are day-to-day money-manifesting techniques to help you remove any limiting beliefs about money, so you can feel extremely abundant, manifest your greatest visions, and live the life you truly want and deserve. Dare to dream.

The goal of this book is for you to completely shift how you live your life. It's time to dedicate yourself to this transformation by changing your habits, behaviors, thought patterns, and attitude so you can start attracting things instantly. The more you increase your vibration and feel good about yourself, the more you'll begin to attract that which matches your frequency. I'll also be teaching you how to trust the process and let go of the need to know "how" things will happen. Nothing is stopping you from having what you want but the things you tell yourself. It's time to boost your energy, change your mindset, and manifest your reality.

Enjoy manifesting!

Love,

Idil Ahmed

1

Manifest Now

What is manifestation?

Manifestation is the ability to attract, create, and turn any vision you have into reality. You can speak, think, feel, and create anything into existence by simply being aware that everything starts with you. You are a powerful being. Your mind is powerful. You are capable of creating the reality you want. The only things that stand in the way of manifesting your dreams are limiting beliefs, ideas, and lack of understanding of what you're capable of doing. This book is going to help you get as clear as possible through learning about your inner powers. It will teach you how to guide them to create the reality you want. Manifesting is not a complicated thing. Once you learn how to remove what is standing in your way, you'll notice that things just begin to flow into your life effortlessly.

One of the things I have discovered during the learning process of manifesting what I want is the importance of now. For so many years, I have heard people say *live in the moment* or *all things happen in the now*. I didn't understand it until I really took a deep look within my own mind and discovered that I would always think of my manifestations as if they were in the future. I had that "one day" mindset trap that we all fall into when we don't analyze our own thought patterns and beliefs. This was an honest, reflective moment for me. I had to be real with myself and declare that I was going to change my mind about the future and focus my mental energy on the moment so I could Manifest Now.

Manifesting now has to do with seeing yourself in the desired state *now*. If you think of it in the future, you won't use the intense emotion of the now, which is the fire that fuels the vision to come to life. You will just hope that it happens instead of knowing that it is happening. Once you make the declaration that you are going to Manifest Now, everything in the universe begins to shift to align to your inner state. So...feel healthy now. Feel abundant now. Feel successful now. Feel beautiful and loved now. Don't wait for it. Feel it into existence. Fully connect your emotion to the vision. Let the joy of it happening *now* fill your mind and body.

To be able to start manifesting now, you have to set the intention that you will manifest everything you want by believing in it. Just being here and reading this is already enough to get the process started. Believe in yourself by taking this step and making the commitment to know what you're capable of. During the process of reading this book, you'll suddenly experience unexpected miracles and blessings. Things will start to happen for you. You will have a lot of clarity and *aha* moments, and everything will start to make sense. There will even be times when you'll be so present, you'll notice the manifestation process and how it all comes together. The wisdom and insight offered in this book will completely change your life.

Begin, at this moment, to feel the energy of endless possibilities. Feel yourself receiving everything your heart desires. This is the energy state you should feel and exist within while reading this book. The possibilities are endless.

Be prepared to change your life. You will need to make the commitment to yourself that you will invest your mental, physical, and spiritual energy into understanding yourself and what you're capable of. This experience is going to require you to be ready to shed old energy patterns, limiting belief systems, negative thinking, and habits that no longer serve you. You have to begin to take control of your life. The things that distract you are only keeping you from realizing the magical results that can occur when you focus your mind and concentrate your thoughts. Make a declaration to yourself right now that you are ready to take back your power and use it to create the life you want. It's time to begin manifesting your greatest dreams. You are powerful!

2

Mental - It All Starts in the Mind

In order to understand your ability to manifest, you must first step back and begin to accept that EVERYTHING starts in your mind. Take a moment to look around yourself, and notice that everything surrounding you was once a thought in your mind. You envisioned yourself having that item before you even went to purchase it. Now, take it a step further, and think about how the items around you were once an idea in someone else's mind to create and bring to life. Everything we do and experience stems from a single thought. The vision comes before materialize into the physical realm. It keeps me inspired to remember that everything starts in the mind. If all that surrounds me was once a vision, what can I do with the same mental power to materialize exactly what I want into the physicalthe physical manifestation. All things in the unseen?

Begin to realize that if everything starts in the mind, then manifesting is your natural birthright. Every single moment, you see images in your mind before you take any kind of action. Sometimes, this happens extremely quickly, and you forget to even be conscious of it. Take a step back for a moment, and notice that when you intend to do something, no matter what it is, you see yourself doing it in your mind first. You play out the whole scene and outcome in your mind before you experience the physical result. Once you agree on a mental scene or image, your physical body goes and performs it. This goes back to the way everything starts in the mind. Be present enough to notice this, and it will further empower you to believe that manifesting is your natural birthright. No matter what you do, you can't do it without imagining it first.

Now that you understand what natural visualization (and experiencing the vision you've imagined) is like on a daily basis, let's take it a step further and discuss the difference between day-to-day manifestations and the big visions you want to attract into your life. When you imagine yourself going to the store to make a purchase, the first thing you do is see yourself getting the items or things you need in your mind. You see the vision, process, and result. You easily get it done without overthinking whether or not it can even happen for you, because you are the one actually doing it. You might not realize it, but this is also considered manifesting. You see the image first, then acquire the physical experience.

When you start to do the same thing with your big dreams, you may start to worry, because you assume the vision isn't attainable since it's not as easy as getting up and driving to the store. Well, let me tell you something: it *is* as easy as that. This is where you need to realize how to surrender to the universe to make the delivery and alignments happen for you, which will require trust. I am sure you've noticed that the things you don't worry about too much manifest faster. You might have a quick thought about it, and then it suddenly happens. This is a glimpse of what is possible for you, and what the universe can do when we don't overthink, worry, or stress about the *how*. We will get into that more in later sections. The whole point is to remember that you are visualizing and imagining what you want to manifest all day long.

Are you consciously or unconsciously creating your reality?

Every single day, whether you are aware of it or not, you are creating your reality. The goal is to start acting as the conscious creator of your reality. When you are unconsciously creating your reality, you assume everything that is happening to you is out of your hands. You think life is random and unpredictable. You assume the challenges affecting your life can't be changed. To unconsciously create your reality is to remain unaware that you have the power to imagine, visualize, speak, and create your experience.

Most people who unconsciously create their reality assume the victim role and the *poor me* mindset. They believe that other people are lucky, and their life is hard. They create a negative mental image and narrative that keeps them in that cycle of lack. Most of their conversations will be very pessimistic, because they have forgotten their innate power as creators of their reality. This attitude of blaming external circumstances and other people is very limiting, and makes people feel like they can't change their lives.

Everything that is happening in your life is in *your* hands. You can change things right now, and never look back. You aren't tied to the past. All those stories and experiences are gone. Who you are today is brand new. The only person who was repeating habits, behaviors, and thought patterns was you. Staying stuck in past *could haves*, *should haves*, and *would haves* only takes away your power and leeches away your life force, which you can use to invest in change today. You have to remember that at each moment, you decide how you'll spend your mental, physical, and emotional energy. What are you giving your attention to?

Nothing in life is random. People can even experience positive results from unconsciously creating their reality, and just calling it luck or coincidence. They don't know that they are co-creating with the universe daily. The point is to start consciously creating and setting your intentions about what you want to manifest.

Being conscious of creating your reality also means taking responsibility for what is happening in your life. In order to attract more effectively, you must pay attention to your actions, habits, and thoughts as well as what you speak into the universe. This new way of thinking and being present will make you feel empowered, inspired, and motivated, no matter what is happening. Those who are consciously creating their reality know that what they intend will manifest. They also know the power of attention, which helps them stay focused on solutions and answers instead of problems and hardship. Conscious creators know exactly how to turn anything that seems negative into a positive opportunity.

As a conscious creator, you have the choice to take full control of your life. As you continue to read this book, you'll start making great changes, and manifesting what you desire. I want you to start noticing how present, involved, and alive your mind is. Your mental energy is waiting for directions. Your mind wants to be guided by you, so it can help you manifest what you want. Don't let external reality and people outside of yourself decide for you what to do with your mind. You are either creating your reality yourself, or other people are doing it for you via influence and suggestion. Being a conscious creator is going to give the power back to you, so you aren't influenced by the limiting thoughts and ideas of others. You'll start to realize who you are and what you can do. Acceptance of this truth right now is already causing immense changes in the way you think and view things. It is not a matter of one day, but rather *right in this moment* that you start to take ownership of your life.

As humans, we have the ability to observe our thoughts as they come into our minds. This is called *metacognition*: the ability to think about thinking. This ability allows you to step back and go within so you can notice your predominant thoughts. You can analyze yourself—and create better for yourself. Being a conscious creator means that you are present enough to analyze yourself. This is the first step in the manifestation process. You have to begin to be more present with yourself, so you can guide your mind to where you would like it to go. After dealing with negative thoughts and a pessimistic attitude, you might feel like you don't know how to tame your mind. However, with daily practice and self-awareness, you can begin to turn things around for yourself.

The more present you become, the more you'll notice which thoughts, habits, and behaviors you need to change. Be honest with yourself about what needs to change. Don't ever say *that's just who I am* when it comes to what isn't serving you or helping you evolve. You are not defined by anything, or limited by past experiences. You can turn things around and change for the better. You can completely recreate your whole life right now. That is the power you have. Don't let the idea of change make you feel uncomfortable. You have to understand that you are starting to completely reprogram how you think, feel, and experience life. Inner work produces the greatest results, and you'll feel more in control of your life by choosing how to respond to things instead of reacting to everything. You'll become more mindful and conscious about everything you say and do.

Now that you are beginning to understand that you are a natural-born manifestor, you can begin to create what you want. At this point, you'll start to consciously think of something you want to manifest and feel that energy entering your life at that moment. In a later section, I'll discuss with you how to visualize and invoke the emotion of what your heart desires.

Before you begin to understand your mental energy, you need to know that your thoughts are a powerful frequency that's constantly being projected into the universe. While you are thinking, you might not see it physically, but your thoughts are present and ready to be directed toward what you want. Just because you can't see something doesn't mean it's not real.

It's also good to notice the kinds of thoughts you predominantly entertain. When you ponder this, you'll notice that these thoughts are the ones you have been manifesting. If you constantly think negatively, you'll notice things always going wrong. If you have a negative view of money and success, you'll create negative experiences that prove to you what you think is real. If you think love is hard to find, that is what you will manifest. Your mind isn't going to create a reality that you don't think about or believe in. Its duty is to show you more of what you think, feel, and say all the time. You are a magnet to your predominant thoughts and habits.

Each time you think something negative, ask yourself: Is this what I want to manifest?

Always remember that your thoughts are powerful, and are constantly being projected into the universe. The more repetitive the thought, the stronger the ability to manifest it becomes; and when thoughts are charged with emotion, they manifest more quickly. Emotions are a powerful energy field, since they are centered in the heart. Research conducted by the HeartMath Institute has shown that the electromagnetic field of the heart expands further than the mind. When you think about something and have an intense emotion behind it, things begin to happen more quickly.

When you really come to see that all begins with the mind, the next step is learning how to focus your mental energy. With all the distractions going on, it is imperative that you train yourself to focus on a single thought for more than 17 seconds. Each day, you can add 10 seconds. You'll gradually gain the ability to stay focused on the vision you want to manifest. The goal in this section is not only to make you more aware of your thoughts and mind power, but also to get you in training mode to exercise your mind's abilities. If you wanted to get fit right now, you would be eating better and consistently working out every day to get the results you want. The mental field is the same. You have to start training yourself to focus on a single thought without distraction. The more you build on this, the better you will become at creating your reality. You will notice yourself ceasing to waste time on frivolous things that once took so much of your energy.

A lot of your energy is wasted daily on things that don't help you create the reality you want. This can include browsing social media all day, texting, watching TV, or doing things that simply don't contribute toward your goal. When you declare something, you must understand how to concentrate on it and get the work done. This is where the majority of your power lies. Each moment, you have a choice about how you use your energy and where to place your attention. Make sure it is benefiting you and serving your greatest vision.

3

Guiding Your Mental Energy

Now that you have learned the power of your mind, you can take the important step of beginning to guide your mental energy toward the reality you want. You will begin the manifestation process by keeping a consistent train of thought through a repetition process. The first step in guiding your mental energy is to recognize what your predominant thoughts are. Are you constantly negative? Do you have a pessimistic attitude about what you can accomplish? Do you believe in yourself?

The goal is to start paying attention to the thoughts you have been giving your mental energy to. Some of these thoughts are only there because you have accepted them as reality, when realistically, they don't belong to you. People assume that thoughts are something they can't change. They feel like they are stuck, because they give more power to the thought than their ability to change it. You can change what you think. You no longer have to be a victim to negative thoughts that don't serve you. Now that you have become aware of the fact that you are in control of the thoughts you allow to stay, you can start changing them into the ones you want.

Be patient with yourself during this process. You are learning new things and taking action to literally create the best life for yourself. To really make lasting changes, one must learn to master the mind in order to guide mental energy toward the desired results. You are about to do just that. You are no longer going to just live life without being aware of who you really are and the powers you have. This is a time for great change, and the discovery of your abilities represents the start of creating abundance, happiness, and freedom. To be free, one must have an open mind. You are becoming more aware of what you can do, and how you can start guiding your mental energy to be more optimistic, positive, and excited about what you're creating.

Take the same energy you use to doubt yourself and invest it in faith.

After you have recognized your predominant thoughts, analyze the results they have gotten you. How has negative thinking or doubting yourself served your life? What has fear created for you? How many of your dreams and ideas have been cut short by worry or lack of faith? These are the kinds of thoughts that stop many people from creating the life they truly want. It's not that something great can't happen for you; it's that you talk yourself out of it, because your thoughts become more real than your vision.

If you have never worked on your mindset, then this will come as a challenge at first. It is a process of reprogramming yourself from limiting beliefs to thoughts of abundance. You have to dedicate yourself to investing in your mind so you can do something you have never done before. Dedicating your time and energy to this will give you the life you want. The reason why many people aren't living the lives they want or manifesting their greatest dreams is because they don't understand that life is a mental game. Everything is about how you think and feel—and what you believe.

Not many people want to invest in change, because it requires them to shed old ways of thinking and living. You have to be okay with being uncomfortable, and face the illusion of what holds you back. When you get your mental state in check, you will notice that things aren't as bad or scary as they seem. You have dared to face yourself, and with that risk comes great rewards. It is up to you, at this moment, to begin to reprogram your mind to thoughts that actually serve you.

If a negative thought comes into your mind, you don't have to identify with it and own it as yours. Simply release it, and replace it with a thought you want. You must do this consistently as you learn how to change your thought patterns. Thoughts are similar to habits. The thoughts you think daily can become dominant if you have been thinking them for a long time. This is why you have to be consistent in using repetition to change your mental habits and create healthier ones. Don't feel discouraged during this transformation process if you are going against limiting beliefs. Your drive to push through is what is going to help you during this manifestation process.

You can recreate yourself and change your life. I did it, and I learned that not giving up or giving in to fear was what got me through. Don't talk yourself out of your change. It is easy to go back to old patterns and be comfortable, just like many people. You're here to own your powers and live life exactly how you want. You are the creator of your universe. You have the power to manifest easily. Once you begin to remove and replace negative thoughts with positive ones, you'll start to notice how effortlessly everything starts to come together. You might even be surprised to notice how quickly your thoughts manifest. You'll be thinking of something, and suddenly, you'll hear someone else talking about it, or you'll start to see it all around you. The more your thoughts and intentions become clarified, the easier they become to manifest.

Remember, manifesting is your natural birthright. This is something you have always been doing, but down the line, you may have picked up on other people's beliefs about life and felt like good things couldn't happen for you. This is an illusion. Those who feel like something is not possible simply don't believe in themselves. Most people learn these limiting beliefs during childhood, when they hear their parents or others talk about lack. Abundance isn't a daily conversation for many people, because they don't know what they are truly capable of. That's what this book is here to teach you: how to remember your natural manifesting abilities and create the best reality for yourself.

Each day, create a mental economy for yourself. How many of your thoughts are actually giving you a return on investment? Your mental energy is an investment in what you want to receive back from the universe. Are you investing in positive thoughts to get positive results? Also, pay close attention to the feelings the thoughts produce. Do you feel good or bad? Do you feel happy or sad? How are your thoughts making you feel? Your emotions are a good indicator of what's happening in your mind. Don't get caught in a negative thought/negative emotion cycle. Know when to snap out of it, and break the cycle by reminding yourself that *you* decide which thoughts you emotionalize and devote your energy to. Invest in positive thoughts daily. Remain hopeful during challenges, even in moments when you feel like doubting yourself.

With all the changes you'll be experiencing, now is the time to share with you how important it is not to be hard on yourself during the process. When you are shifting mentally, a lot of changes can happen on an energetic level. The clearing of old thought patterns and old ways of thinking can take a lot of energy, which is why I recommend getting rest when you need to, and taking care of your physical wellness. You don't always have to be on the go doing something.

Take some time to rest and recover. You don't always have to be so busy, or pushing yourself so hard. Step back and take care of yourself. These moments of self-care will add value, energy, purpose, and creativity to everything you do. Find a healthy balance, and enjoy your life.

There needs to be balance. Take time to nurture your mental, physical, and spiritual wellness. When you start to change negative thoughts to positive ones, you'll realize that the old thought patterns might come back to test you and make you doubt yourself. The test is to see if you actually have succeeded in your transformation. This is when you will have to be firm and face fear head on. The illusion is only in the mind. Thoughts that try to talk you out of your changes are your past negative thinking trying to find a space to live and survive again. You must not fall for that trap or return to that draining cycle of doubt. You must step outside of your comfort zone, and walk your path with an inner faith that all is going to happen for you.

Even when things seem to be falling apart, you must still have unwavering faith that everything is working in your favor. This is an important tip to remember when guiding your mental energy. When it comes to manifesting what you want, your vision is more important than your reality. When you keep believing, visualizing, and thinking positively, all things will begin to align for you. Your faith is in the unseen. Remember, everything in life starts in the mind as a vision. Stay strong during the process, and keep reminding yourself that all is mental.

4

Use Your Mental Energy to Your Advantage

Since you have learned how to guide your mental energy toward the things you want and the way you want to feel, it's now time to actually start using your mental energy to create your reality. What do you want to manifest? Ask yourself that question. *If I could have anything I wanted in this universe, and it could show up in my life right now, what would I want?* When you think about this question, be completely free. Do you want to manifest financial freedom? A relationship? A job? Better connections? Better opportunities? A vacation? More blessings? All of this is possible for you. What you want already exists, and it is waiting for you to align with it.

You must declare that you are ready to receive. The reason I ask you to think about what you want is because most people have no clue what they really want out of life. Even if they do, they think it's not possible. These limiting thoughts are what hold people back. If someone else on this earth can have the things you want, then that is an example that it's possible for you to have them, too. What did they do to get them? They aren't any different from you. They just applied the manifesting tools and believed in themselves until they manifested what they wanted. Most successful people will tell you to believe in yourself and be consistent. You have to start trusting in your vision to create the reality you want.

I have read some powerful books, and they all have one thing in common: what you believe in matters more than what you're experiencing. You can start the process by creating a manifestation journal. This is your personal journal in which you will write exactly what you want to manifest. I don't want you to think about how this will happen for you. I don't even want you to worry about when it will happen. I just want you to freely write exactly what it is that you want to create in your reality.

When you are writing in your manifestation journal, charge your writing with the energy that it is about to happen for you right now. Write *Manifest Now* in big letters at the top of each page. I remember I did that in my manifestation journal, and quickly started seeing results. I have always believed in the power of writing down my visions. I usually write mine in the style of a letter to the universe, commanding all the things I want to come find me quickly, easily, and effortlessly. When you are writing in your manifestation journal, invoke emotions. How would you feel if everything you wrote down manifested for you? Feel that feeling as you are writing your visions and goals. Smile while you're doing it. This is a great way to energize your manifestation journal so you'll believe and know that everything you have written is about to happen for you. I always like to think, feel, and celebrate as if I have already manifested what I want. This is a great way to raise your vibration so you can start the aligning process.

Another great way to manifest what you want is by visualizing it. Images are a powerful way to create what you want, because we are imaginative creatures. We don't think in words; we see images in our minds. Visualization is a great tool to use, because you already do it anyway. You either think about the past or go into the future with your mind.

I want you to combine your manifestation journal with visualizations. Each day, look at the things you want to manifest and create a vision for them. See yourself in your mind's eye actually having the experience you've written down. Say that you want to manifest money, and see yourself getting unexpected payments into your bank account. Feel the energy of money surrounding you. Visualize yourself holding a large amount (I'll be going further into money manifestation in the Magnetic Money Mindset section.) If you want to manifest your dream home, see yourself walking through the home.

When it comes to visualizing, be as detailed as possible. Have fun with it. See your furniture, your interior design, and yourself living there. Another thing that can help you get clear in your vision is to go look at your dream home. Search homes that are for sale, and print images of the ones you like. Keep the design of the house and the experience of living there fully present within your mind. When you are visualizing, find a quiet place where you won't be disturbed, and create a mental movie of what you want. If you want to manifest a healthy relationship, see yourself in your mental movie with someone with all the traits you like. Feel happy, as if all of this is actually happening for you. If you feel funny and silly doing this, remind yourself that you are a powerful being who is already visualizing and creating mental movies. All you're doing is creating what you want consciously.

Keep watching your mental movies until they become clear and easy to walk through. Imagine your mental movies like a virtual reality of the life you want to live. Your mind doesn't know if what you are imagining is actually happening or if you are just pretending. This is why, when you see something that looks like an insect or snake, you might freak out; and later, when you know it is not, you calm down. If your mind knew it was a false alarm, it would not have overreacted out of fear. However, you could have made yourself believe that it was an insect or a snake when it was just a piece of stick. This is why what you believe and envision matters more than reality. Your mind will believe what you tell it, and create that experience for you. So keep visualizing what you want to manifest.

If you have a hard time initially focusing on your mental movie, you can use a vision board to help you see the images more clearly. A vision board is a tool used to help clarify, concentrate, and maintain your focus on a specific life goal. Literally, a vision board is any sort of board on which you display images that represent whatever you want to be, do, or have in your life. This allows your brain to capture the images and words to trigger a mood and a feeling. Image + emotion = creation of an experience. Seeing your vision board daily will shift your mind and start aligning you with these experiences in ways you can't even imagine. This is why you shouldn't be too concerned with "how" it will happen. Trying to use your conscious mind will only limit you to what you already know, but allowing your subconscious mind to guide you in the right direction will bring you unlimited opportunities. You just have to trust the process. You might suddenly meet someone, or go someplace that aligns you with a connection you need to reach your goal.

I remember after I started working on my manifestation journal and creating mental movies daily, I got results in ways I can't even put into words. The universe and the power of the source is something I don't think we can fully grasp. I like to not know how, because this allows the universe to deliver more quickly and efficiently. If I thought about it too much, I would limit it based upon whom I know and what I know. However, when I decide to surrender to the universe, I start tuning into a greater frequency that aligns and connects everyone and everything. I meet the perfect person at the right time. I show up somewhere at the exact moment to find the answer to something I need to know.

It's like you are being guided to receive what you want. Manifesting is no joke. The power of your mind is no joke. I realized this when I looked back at my manifestation journal and saw that I had literally manifested everything I had written there. I even looked at my vision board, and was blown away by the results. Sometimes, we get so busy creating the next thing, we forget we have already manifested almost everything we have yearned for. I like to look back at my older manifestation journals and use them as inspiration for my next vision and goal.

Remember to stay focused and consistent. The reason most people don't accomplish their goals is because they're not a primary focus; they look at it as a "one day" scenario. However, every moment is a chance to impress upon your mind exactly what you want. The vision board allows you to maintain focus, and acts as a constant reminder to your mind's eye. This can be a great tool for you to add into your life to bring clarity, focus, and purpose to the achievement of your greatest desires. Also, the more specific you are about what you want, the higher your chances of receiving exactly what you asked for. Saying something like, "I want a better life!" is not enough. What does a better life mean to you? What would you be doing? Where would you be? Who would you be with? How would you be feeling? Be detailed. Be specific. Your dreams are waiting for you to shift your mind to see them.

5

The Inner Love Flow

Relationships play a vital role in our lives. For the longest time, I have received so many questions from many people who want to know how they can manifest the right partner or how they can create a healthier bond within the relationship they already have. Some people are going through a break-up or a divorce and want to start over. It's never too late. My intention of this chapter is really for you to discover your own essence. I'm sure you've heard "love yourself" so many times before, but what does that even mean? How can you truly love yourself if you haven't learned how to cultivate a healthier mindset and a real connection within your soul? Self-love stems from knowing that you are already whole. God gives you unconditional love with every breath you take. Somewhere down the line in life, you have probably forgotten this flow that already belongs to you. The love flow, which is constantly pouring into you never stops providing for you. Sometimes we have to get out of our minds for a moment and simplify life. Love is given freely and unconditionally to us. When we forget this connection, we start to feel like we need to receive it from the outside. When the focus becomes external in receiving love, a lot of problems start to occur. When one feels empty on the inside because they have forgotten their own connection, they begin to get into a state of desperation and neediness. This yearning for fulfillment turns into a need for validation and approval.

Never seek validation, approval or acceptance. Love yourself instead. Give yourself the attention you need. Go within and dive deeper until you realize that everything you've always been looking for was only to get closer to your own self. You need you more than you need anyone else.

In order to accept your inner bliss and recognize the love flow in your life, you first have to be honest with yourself about the things that are holding you back. Guilt and blame lowers your frequency. It is so easy to point the finger and blame others. It is so easy to think that other people are doing you wrong. The most powerful thing you can start doing right now is to take responsibility for your own life. You are the creator of all your experiences. Today is the day where all blame comes to an end. Your power is recognizing that you can manifest exactly what you want in a relationship by continually growing from the past and learning the lessons that will help you improve.

When someone has forgotten their inner love flow, they start to look for that fulfillment on the outside, which leads to conditional love. Everything about the relationship becomes how can you get something back form what you give. The lack of understanding where your source of inner love stems from puts you in a position to always seek to receive. Feeling empty and being unsure leads to being desperate and needing constant validation. When you love yourself, you also feel good about yourself. Have you noticed when you chase people they run away? Have you also noticed that when you refocus your energy on yourself and your growth, the person comes running back? What is happening energetically? What shifted? Everything takes place on an energy level first. You are constantly sending out how you think and feel into the universe, which is picked up by other people on a subtle level. If you feel desperate and needy, your energy is usually low, and in that state, you'll do many things that compromise your integrity and truth. You don't have to send a hundred texts or calls to get attention. You don't have to do things on social media to prove a point. Each time you plot something to get attention from someone you end up actually feeling depleted because you're still paying them your most valuable asset; your attention. You don't need to play any games. You need to do better. You need to get better. What you really need is a redirection of your focus and a rediscovering of your inner values.

Everything changes when you begin to love yourself. You no longer send out energy of desperation or need to be filled from the outside. You become a powerful source within yourself that attracts better. The more you love who you are, the less you seek validation and approval.

You have to always remember that you are the value. You are the gift. You are special. Never allow yourself to feel so low that someone who also doesn't feel good about themselves takes advantage of your weak moment. This insight is meant to lift you higher so that you can release the energy of needing external validation to feel worthy. Once you discover this inner love flow, you'll never again get caught up in those states of losing yourself in something that doesn't have long-term benefits.

When someone hasn't discovered their love flow, they start to attract other people who also haven't made that discovery. The whole point of the attraction is to show you the reality you created, and if you don't like what you see, you can go back and recreate it. Failed relationships were only there to help you grow so that you can discover what you actually want and deserve. It ended so you can enter the next phase of your evolution.

Billions of humans exist on the planet. So many incredible people that you haven't met yet. Why limit your experience to a few bad interactions and assume that greatness doesn't roam the earth. All is possible for you. Switch your mindset so that new energy can enter your life.

Never be afraid to let go of something that's past its due date. Way too many people stay in toxic relationships out of fear that they can't get better. You know when something is done. Usually, if you're growing and know that it's over don't give yourself excuses. If the first thought that comes to your mind is that you might not find better or you don't know what's next then it's time to actually take action and let go. Don't stay out of fear. Don't make excuses for yourself. This is your one life, and you must fully live it.

Once you start to validate yourself and understand that you are worthy already you'll begin to operate at a frequency of love that will fill you up and make you whole. Your life will start changing because you're no longer chasing, trying so hard, and living in fear. Your attention is going to be focused back on yourself so that you can discover how to give love without needing it from the outside.

If you're already in a relationship and want to grow with your partner, then you also need to understand how to give unconditional love. All mistakes need to be faced directly and forgiven quickly. Holding onto the past and constantly bringing it up is draining to you and your partner. You have to keep your inner thoughts about your partner positive. Whether you understand it or not, you're always telepathically communicating with your partner. If you've been with your partner longer, the telepathic communication is even stronger, but nevertheless, it is always happening between all people. Many people feel and think negatively about their partner, and that energy is felt.

Send love to someone who hurt you through a prayer so that you can break free from the pain. Each time you elevate above the past, you win.

Understand that it is not only what you're saying, but also what you're thinking that has the power. The thoughts you're having about your relationship are affecting the results you're getting from your partner.

The reason why most relationships or marriages don't last is because of the inner thoughts that we choose to entertain can either help us or hurt us. Let's say your partner upsets you, and you pretend that "you're over it" externally, but internally, you're constantly repeating to yourself what they've done to you with anger, resentment, fear, sadness, or just pure frustration. You're probably having an inner dialect saying, "they'll just do it again" or "why do they keep doing this" or many of the other negative repetitive thoughts. On the outside, you're playing it cool, but internally you're upset with them. This hiding of real feelings starts to build up and cause other problems. This is what makes the couple drift apart, eventually ending the relationship.

What most don't realize is how powerful those silent thoughts can be. Instead of breaking each other down, why not uplift and heal with your mind. A great awareness to have is, what you think of your partner, they become. You will see more of the traits, habits, beliefs, and actions you do, or don't like about them. It all depends on where you put your mind. Create healthy thoughts about your partner; say sweet loving words about them to yourself. Appreciate their smallest effort; give them reminders of how you feel, be more expressive to one another. Have the thoughts you had about them when you first fell in love. When you're having a negative thought about them, ask yourself, do I want to manifest this in my relationship?

The inner world influences the outcome of your relationship. Each thought you send out can be a powerful energy that can align you and your partner to create a healthier relationship. Most people who don't know this, struggle in their relationship because they don't understand the power of their thoughts, words, and emotions. What you think internally, you see externally. Let love power your relationship.

Sending Love Experiment

If you're in a relationship, I want you to try something that has been working for many people I work with. For one week, I want you to focus your mindset and energy on everything that is positive and loving about your partner. You can do this longer but one week is a start to activate and change your inner world. This sending love experiment will start to shift you and your relationship for the better.

1. Mentally forgive your partner for all their past mistakes. The whole point is to start changing your inner world so that you don't hold any resentment. Whatever comes to your mind that triggers an intense negative emotion you can clear it out by saying "I forgive you _____ (name) for _____ (behavior/action)!" Feel yourself genuinely letting go of it all and being at peace with yourself. This is a healing step so that you can let go of the past. Your relationship is new every day. You don't need to bring the past up anymore. Forgive and move forward.

2. Bring up positive memories that you had with your partner in your mind. Take some time to enjoy the feeling the positive memories ignite within you. Smile knowing how much you love this person and how much joy you share with them. Remember all the good times you had with them. Remember how you felt when you first met them.

3. Send them love and positive thoughts. This is a vital part of the experiment. For one whole week send your partner love. Even if they live with you send them love through your mind. See them being filled with so much love and support. You can visualize this happening. In your mind see your partner smiling and hugging you. Visualize so much love and happiness between you guys. Also, if any negative thoughts come up banish them and replace them with a more positive loving thought. This is a start to change the inner world to be more in the love flow. The endless love pouring into you from the source is being spread with your thoughts and emotions.

4. Let your inner world align with your outer world. You'll become more at ease in this experiment because you know your love comes from the source. You don't need to try so hard to get attention from your partner. Instead feel yourself being filled and full of love. Ironically when you are so full of love, your partner will be more attracted to you. Love is the highest frequency and attracts everything. When you radiate inner love and peace, you'll find yourself attracting more of that from your environment.

5. Let your actions show that you are free, relaxed and yourself. This experiment will not only create better harmony between you and your partner, but it will also allow you to be at peace with yourself. During this week, focus on encouraging your partner. Be supportive. Be loving. Say things you normally don't say. Do things you normally don't do.

6. Let your mindset be focused on solutions this week. If a problem comes up, find out how you can communicate about it. Find out what is the solution that can make it better. Don't hold onto things for long either, solve it quickly and move forward. The more you practice looking for solutions, the easier it will be to solve problems.

This sending love experiment is supposed to help you release, think, and feel love surrounding all aspects of your life. While it can help your relationship, it will also help you become more aware of your predominate inner thoughts and emotions. The whole point of the love flow is open your heart and remember your true essence so that you can be filled by the source.

If you're single, don't let yourself feel pressured by society or others who are constantly asking about your relationship status or when you'll be getting married. No matter how old you are, it is never too late to find love. Your time is coming because you will manifest the partner that is aligned with your highest ideals. The most important thing is being right within so that you are aware enough to know what you want and what you deserve. It's not about just being in a relationship; it is about being whole and healthy mentally, emotionally and spiritually so that you can create a fulfilling experience with someone that enriches your soul.

The first thing you need to start doing right away is discovering what it is that you want in a partner. So many people will tell you 101 things they don't want in a partner but don't fully speak and think about what kind of person they want to align with. Each time you say what you don't want you're actually giving your attention and focus to that. Your thoughts are powerful. You need to focus on the kind of partner you want to manifest instead.

Manifesting Your Partner Experiment

You can manifest someone into your life just like you manifest anything else. The universe has a way of aligning us with people we share common thought waves with. If your mindset during this experiment is focused on what you want instead of what you don't want, you'll start to create a vortex of energy that aligns you with the right one. This experiment is all about having fun and enjoying your life. It is not about being desperate and constantly wondering when this person will show up. Desperation repels what you want. You must have faith that it is happening for you and that it will work out. The best things in life happen when you least expect it. Let this be a guiding thought as you being the manifesting your partner experiment.

The first thing I want to share with you before we dive deep into this is that you must be that which you want to attract. You must hold the thought pattern, beliefs, and feeling of whom you want to manifest. People align because they share some kind of core values and thought patterns that resonate. Become who you want to manifest. Expose your attention and awareness to that kind of person. Who do you know has the qualities you want in a partner. See yourself allowing those core values to resonate with you. Another major tip I have for you is being happy for married people. Be happy for people in a relationship. What you want for others is what you get for yourself. Never wish bad on someone just because you don't have something. This is a kind of energy that also repels from you what you want to manifest. Joyously celebrate other people's happiness. Also, watch love movies and listen to music that encourages relationships, happiness, unity, and upliftment. All of this is to help you switch your focus and attention to the love frequency. What you focus on will find you.

You don't have to do anything special but be yourself and be happy. You don't need to try hard or go out of your way to seek attention. Your glow comes from loving yourself and knowing that everything starts with you.

1. Make a list of everything you want in a partner. What are the qualities you value? If you had your ideal partner right now, what would he or she be like? Be very detailed in your list. Also, invoke the emotion that each quality would bring you if it were manifested in a partner that's standing in front of

you right now. How would it feel? Connecting the emotion with the words is a powerful way to charge your list so that you are constantly reminded of what you are about to manifest. Make sure that you write this list on a paper that you can either carry in your bag or wallet. Read the list daily and celebrate the arrival of your partner.

2. Be open to unexpected invitations and sudden encounters. The whole point is to remove how you think it will happen and allow yourself to be guided by the universe. Don't let yourself even try to be concerned with how and when. Surrender and let it be. Have fun and be friendly.

3. Images are a powerful way to connect with an experience. You can add images to your vision board that supports your desired relationship. If you want to get married, then plan your wedding in your man-ifestation journal. Put yourself in the energy state as if everything already happened.

4. Thank the universe for you healthy loving relation-ship. This energy of being grateful keeps you in the frequency of love.

5. Keep your mind free of doubt.

Now that you are in the love flow, you'll start to notice a shift within yourself that's more at ease instead of looking and searching desperately. You are just being, and that is the state you should be in to welcome new energy and new experiences.

Being positive and loving yourself is a daily commitment.

Whether you are single or in a relationship, keep

your mindset clear of negative influences. So many people will create stories in their head about what relationships are like based on what someone else is going through. If someone you know is dealing with infidelity in their relationship, that doesn't mean you have to personalize what they are going through. The whole concepts of all men are one way, or all women are a certain way is causing you to form belief systems that aren't realistic. There are many people who are honest and real. One experience or one headline shouldn't make you generalize populations of people. What you give your focus to will manifest. The conversations you mostly have will become real. It is your duty as a conscious being to start being aware on a daily basis what you consume. The outside reality can influence you if you do not have strong foundation within your own self. It doesn't have to happen to you too. Don't internalize things. Don't personalize them.

Remember that you don't own anyone. Nobody belongs to you in this life. We're all just having an experience together and sharing life with one another. The only things we keep are memories. Make sure you make them worthwhile. You'll feel so free when you can just love without having to possess your partner or control them. Every person is here for a reason. Every person has something to contribute to the world. The more you can support your partner's dreams and visions as you are living yours, the better you'll both feel. Encourage one another to go out there and be the best. We're not here to be boxed in. We're here to experience, love and thrive. Besides all the noise of life, we have to elevate ourselves to remember that everything is momentary. Think about the many people who have transcended and how many people wish they treated them differently or even wished they had said something kind to them. You can do that in your life with all people. Treat them well. Be fully present and loving. Be kind.

6

Letting Go — Allowing — Trusting Phase

Letting go, being patient, allowing, and trusting the process is the most important part of manifesting. Once you have set the intention and created the vision in your mind, start letting go of the need to force it to happen. Remember that your thoughts and emotions are energy, leaving your body to align you and bring you exactly what you need. If you know that you have sent the signal out, then let it go. Believe that what you have been visualizing and writing in your manifestation journal is on the way.

Look at this like placing an order on Amazon. You know that your order is going to arrive. You put in the order to the universe with your thoughts and emotions; trust that it is going to be delivered to you. You wouldn't worry about how Amazon is going to make the delivery, or what kind of truck they will use to bring your package. You don't even care how they bring it. You just know and trust that they will. This is the same way you can start to trust the universe. Put in your order with your mind and emotions. Feel it getting ready to happen for you. Feel it entering your life. Feel the delivery on the way. Get as excited as if you were expecting a big delivery.

Understand that patience is crucial during this time. Being patient and trusting the process means you believe you'll receive the seed you've sown. Don't let worry, fear, or anxiety make you dig up what you've planted just to see if it's growing.

You have to learn to respect and honor the process. When it comes to our goals and dreams, we expect things to happen, like, yesterday. And when they don't show up in the timeline we want or the way we expect, our doubts and limiting beliefs come into play. Our negative mind chatter creeps up and starts blurring our vision. You have to believe that life is perfect, and timing is life's best friend. Trust the process, and have faith in the unseen. The minute you decide on a goal or have a strong vision about what you want to accomplish, the energy starts moving through you and begins the work. Everything is in fruition. Your vision will be realized. Just believe!

During this phase, the universe will start to give you signs and align you with people who will assist you during the process. Be on the lookout for signs about the action you need to take. When an opportunity shows up, take it. Sometimes, you can be manifesting so effortlessly that you might even forget that you wanted to manifest what you are experiencing. I am sure there have been times in the past when you've wanted something so badly, and then it happened. Looking back, you might not even remember that you manifested it, because it came into your life naturally.

Be present enough to notice the signs, and also to listen to your inner guidance. Sometimes, you might be guided to an event and not even know why you're going there; but by the end of the evening, you've met someone who is a good contact to align you with someone else. If you hadn't trusted your inner guidance and gone out instead of staying in, that could have been a missed opportunity. Don't worry, though—the universe is clever, and will always continue to align you. The only difference in how long it takes depends upon how clear you are in tuning into your inner guidance and trusting the process without doubt. At the end of the day, you're always going to manifest what you want if you are persistent enough and believe in what is possible for you.

What can you do to get closer to your vision? You must begin to surround yourself with the frequency, environment, and people who share the vibration of the lifestyle and success you want. I usually use books as mentors. I read autobiographies of the greats, or books on business that help my mind and energy align with what I want to manifest. As you are in the letting-go and trusting phase, you must also be active in immersing yourself in the frequency you want to attract. If you want to manifest financial freedom and don't know anything about starting a business, that's a good time to start learning and trusting the universe to make good business contacts for you.

It's kind of like meeting the right person at the right time. We are all connected, and when we put a vision into our minds, the universe does everything to make it a reality. There are no barriers or blocks. It does happen, and it will happen for you. Be at ease during the process of patiently waiting for your manifestation. Trust that it is on the way. Keep telling yourself to be cool about it. When you are relaxed, your energy is in a more trusting state. When you are stressed, you want to force things to happen, and this causes delays. Strengthen your faith by believing that everything your heart desires is on the way.

7

Physical — Optimize Your Physical Body for More Energy

Are you energized and ready to manifest? As you work on the mental energy to manifest what you want, you must also remember how important it is to have physical energy. When you feel good about yourself, you are happier, more creative, and ready to receive. The goal is to raise your vibration: not only on the mental plane, but on the physical, as well.

Having energy is important in this world. We know that health and wellness are key to an optimal life. When you have more energy, you can do more creative work and feel confident in your ability to produce. If you feel tired and don't take care of yourself, your confidence in yourself will be lower. You have to take care of your physical body so you can pull in more universal energy to create the reality you want. It's crucial to know the importance of deep breathing, spending time in nature, and consuming nutrient-dense foods. There are several ways to raise your physical energy, and the first step is to be real with yourself about what you consume. Think about what you put into your body. Is it giving you more energy, or is it making you tired and depleted?

Energy State and Nourishment

The fastest way to increase your vibration is to consume food that's filled with vital energy. Energy is the core substance of everything in the universe. Without energy, there would be no life. Understanding how energy frequencies work is important for your well-being, because when your energy isn't vibrating correctly, you are more vulnerable to disease, negative thinking, and feeling down. Plants are filled with vital energy from the sun, which your body naturally understands. The more you consume nutrient-dense foods, the more positive, energized, and vital you'll feel. My thoughts, my body, and my mind have transformed ever since I implemented nutrient-dense foods in my diet.

The higher your energy, the more you can do. This is why it's important to understand the benefits of everything you consume. Green vegetables and leafy greens are wonderful for your energy state. They contain chlorophyll, which absorbs sunlight—and we know how powerful the sun's energy is! The cells of plants are like batteries that can instantly rev up your body's energy. Other great energy boosters with chlorophyll include wheatgrass, sprouts, spirulina, and blue-green algae. Fruits freshly picked from trees also contain high energy, since they get the full benefit of sunlight. Eating them raw or juicing them can instantly raise your vibration.

Throw dark leafy greens into the juicer or blender, and out comes an easy-to-drink, easy-to-digest, immediately-absorbed energy source. This, above all else, is my favorite way to raise my energy and awareness through food. When I feel low on energy, I make one of these smoothies or juices, and I instantly feel the difference. You'd be surprised at how delicious and satisfying juices and smoothies can be.

There are also a lot of healthy recipe books that can give you thousands of nutrient-dense meals to make on your journey to switching up your lifestyle. Always find out what works for you, and how you can make changes that naturally support your body and well-being.

When I eliminated foods high in sugar and all things processed, my mental state changed. I did a lot of research to discover what worked best for my body. You can do the same. Spend a day figuring out what you want to remove, and what you want to add into your diet. The first step is eliminating processed foods and anything high in sugar, which zaps your energy. We all naturally and intuitively know what isn't good for us and what works well for us. Trust your inner guidance when it comes to what resonates with your body. Different things work for different people.

The results I got after eliminating processed foods and sugar and introducing food from the earth such as fruits, vegetables, nuts, and seeds were tremendously different. I saw that I had more clarity, inner peace, and happiness. I also noticed that I was more creative and energized. Mental fog and lack of focus disappear when you eliminate foods that don't provide you with any nutritional value. It is very important to take care of your physical body during this process of manifesting what you want. The more you step it up in all areas of your life, the more you can do for yourself and others. Take these steps today to start increasing your vibration and realigning with yourself. Feed your body the best foods. Nourish yourself, and know that everything you put inside should be adding to your wellness and energy.

My Personal Wellness Routine

I will share with you my personal routine that helps keep my vibration up. Hopefully, this will help you during your manifestation process.

First things first. I love green smoothies and juices. I will share with you a recipe I make on a consistent basis to keep my energy high. I usually start my morning with visualization and deep breathing. I command my day, and speak health, happiness, peace, love, and blessings over my experience. I made it a habit to focus my energy to speak my day into existence.

Avoid looking at your phone when you wake up. Texts, emails, and social media can wait. You need to prioritize *you*, and give yourself sacred space to be with yourself before you begin your day. Don't say you don't have time, either—you can always make time for what you truly want to do. Now is the time to create healthy habits.

After I am done commanding my day, I start by drinking hot water and lemon. After that, I wait 30 minutes and make my breakfast, which is a powerful green smoothie, rich and jam-packed with nutrients. Morning is a great time for me, because I start my day visualizing what I want to experience and filling my body up with universal energy through deep breathing. I also try to read for 15 to 30 minutes to get my mind and energy aligned with what I want to experience and manifest. I always remind myself that my attention is my power, and I use my personal morning time to empower myself. Once I have taken care of myself mentally, I start the process of nourishing my body.

As I have mentioned, I drink a powerful green smoothie for breakfast. Check out my recipe below. I also make salads, plant-based dishes, and plenty of juices throughout the day to keep me going. I follow a plant-based diet, which I discovered works best for me. Please do what works best for your body. You are intuitive, and once you clear out the junk, you will begin to discover what kinds of food benefit you the most. The recipe I have shared below will serve as an added bonus in your diet, so you, too, can have a nutrient-packed smoothie.

My Favorite Green Smoothie Recipe

Green Kale, Purple Kale, Mixed Sprouts, Cucumber, Rainbow Chard, Rainbow Carrots, Spinach, Arugula, Spring Mix, Avocado, Chia Seeds, Lecithin Powder, Chlorella Powder, Spirulina Powder, Maca Powder, Garden of Life™ Vanilla Protein Powder, and Apple Juice.

During the process of optimizing your physical body, be sure to add new and healthy recipes into your diet. When you are prepared, you have a better chance of succeeding. Do your research, and have fun when it comes to mixing things up and trying a variety of dishes. You'll find plenty of healthy meals when you invest in your physical wellness. Enjoy being optimal!

8

Five Ways to Raise Your Vibration During the Manifestation Process

Raising your vibration means eliminating anything and everything that drains your energy or makes you feel low. It's so important to understand that your vibration is the inner frequency you hold which aligns you with your outer reality. Science has proven that nothing is solid, and that everything is energy vibrating at varying frequencies.

Understanding how energy works will increase the quality of your life. When you feel good or happy, you attract positive experiences. When you feel down or low, you attract negative experiences. Learning how to keep your vibration high is knowing that you have the power to change how you experience your life. When you are in a high-vibrational state, you are much more connected to your inner self, and your primary focus is to live a purposeful, loving, and meaningful life. Learning to eliminate what's keeping you stagnant will free up your energy to reach the next level of your growth.

Mental Cleanse

Doing a mental cleanse involves being conscious of the thoughts to which you give your energy, and actively eliminating those that don't serve you. It is so important to do a mental cleanse as often as possible to increase your vibration. Your mind is the number one place where your energy can be zapped or lowered. This can happen through negative thoughts, overthinking, or being pessimistic about what you can accomplish. If your thoughts are constantly taking you to the past, where you feel regret or pain about something that has happened to you, then it is time to start forgiving yourself so you can be free from it. You have to forgive others, too—for your own mental well-being. You can't carry the burden of playing the same thing over and over again mentally, even though you're no longer going through it physically. Release yourself from it, and free up some energy to start investing in your growth.

A big part of the mental cleanse is realizing that what you give your attention to is either helping you increase your vibration or lowering your energy. The news can be a big trigger for a lot of people, causing them to feel fearful, sad, or angry about what is going on in the world. Yes, there are so many things happening—but we have to remember that in order to make a global impact, we must begin to make personal changes in our own lives. How can we change the world if we are constantly projecting fear, negativity, and hopelessness? It is our duty to be responsible for our own energy state and how it affects the collective. Once we are in harmony with the energy of peace and love, we can actually tune into a state that offers solutions on a global level.

With this understanding, you can start analyzing the other ways you're currently using your mental energy. Do you constantly tune into drama? What do you do with your spare time? Do you focus on personal development and self-improvement? You truly have the choice to do anything you want with your time. How you use that energy determines the results you get out of life. Mentally start tuning into what makes you feel good. Say kind words to yourself. Listen to music that makes your soul move. Watch movies that bring happiness and joy to your life. Have enriching conversations with yourself and others. As you start to do what makes you happy, you'll start feeling your energy go up. Once you feel good about yourself, the universe quickly begins to respond to your frequency.

Spend Time in Nature

I love spending time in nature, because it connects me to the highest frequency and energy of the earth. I feel grounded and more abundant. One thing I love doing is seeing the abundance that surrounds me. There is no limitation in nature. You can find different designs, colors, and beauty everywhere. Nature reminds me that there is no shortage of abundance. The Creator is the best designer and giver of life and beauty. I always affirm *I am abundant* as I walk through nature. I also walk barefoot to connect directly with the earth. If you can, go out into nature as often as possible. Spend time near the water, trees, and wilderness. You will be cleansed and renewed by the powerful energy contained within those spaces. Nature is powerful. It speaks a language that doesn't require words. Getting away from your busy life will help you connect with your soul and release anything keeping you resistant to the flow of life.

Nature releases powerful negative ions that enhance mood, stimulate the senses, and improve overall wellness. Negative ions increase your brainwaves, which results in a higher level of awareness. When you're out in nature, high levels of oxygen are absorbed into the blood cells and oxidize serotonin. Negative ions are considered a natural healer and mood enhancer, and are most commonly found near mountains, lakes, oceans, forests, waterfalls, and less-populated environments with lots of plants. I'm sure you know how great you feel after spending some time in nature. Make it a habit to go out there as much as possible. Connect back with nature; connect back with yourself.

Say Nothing Negative for 24 Hours

Saying nothing negative for 24 hours will help you become more conscious about the things you say to yourself and to others. This is a wonderful exercise that you can do by yourself or with someone else. A lot of the time, we don't even realize how many negative things we say. Always keep the power of your words in mind.

You speak everything you say into existence. When I first decided to do this exercise, I noticed I was more present and conscious when I spoke to others, and even in my own inner dialogue. So many times, I have had conversations with people who spoke negatively about themselves and their goals. I would always remind them to be aware of the words they were choosing to speak into reality. Words have a powerful frequency behind them. They carry an energy that can alter your reality completely. This all depends on the words you are primarily using to express yourself. Are you using words that can help you or harm you? Once you become aware of this power, you'll start using it to change your life.

All your conversations should be empowered by this thought: *I am going to speak what I want to manifest.* One cool thing I like to do is help guide conversations into a positive space. When someone is complaining, I always ask him or her to tell me what they want to manifest instead. I help them take their thoughts out of what is wrong, so they can direct their energy toward what they actually want. This is a tip you can also use with others during your 24-hour exercise of saying nothing negative.

Always remember that the power of sound is conditioning your mind to constantly experience what you speak. The words you speak to others (or yourself) can actually weaken your vibration and cause you not to feel good. Your words guide your mind and body toward the experiences you want to have. This is why, when you speak kind words, everything starts to make you feel good. The energy is attracting itself. During your 24 hours, start saying more kind things to yourself and others. Use your words to empower yourself. Affirm exactly what you want to experience. Change the words you speak, and everything around you will change.

The goal of this exercise is for you to be mindful of your inner dialogue and the conversations you have with others. This is an exercise you can do as often as you like until you get good at speaking what you want into existence on a consistent basis. Remember, you are always giving life to the things you want to manifest through your words.

Accomplish the Goals You Set for Yourself

Learning to accomplish the goals you set for yourself will easily increase your vibration. I'm sure you're familiar with the feeling of joy and happiness you get when you've accomplished a goal. It is such a powerful feeling to know that you can do anything by taking action. However, many people set goals for themselves and never accomplish them. Each time you don't accomplish a goal, you start to feel badly about yourself. This is how negative thoughts and doubt start to seep in, possibly making you feel like you're not good enough. To initiate a shift in your energy state, start setting goals you know you will accomplish. This will help you build momentum, and it will actually make you feel good about yourself. Set daily, monthly, quarterly, and annual goals you know you'll accomplish. Start taking action, and you'll see your life transform.

Self-Care/Self-Love

Self-love is the highest frequency for attracting to you everything you want. When you declare that you want better through action, the universe shows up to guide you in receiving what you want. Self-care is a form of self-respect. Give yourself the space to get clear about what you want. Taking time for yourself doesn't mean that you don't care about others. You have to be your greatest for yourself first, *before* you can give back to others. When you are in this transformative phase, your mind and body are going through a lot of changes. You are relearning how to guide your mental energy and use it to manifest what you want. This is where it becomes crucial to spend more time taking care of yourself, so you can be very clear about your visions.

Self-care is about taking care of your mind, body, and spirit. Do something that makes you feel good and relaxed. A massage is a great way to take care of your body while also promoting a relaxed state. I like to use my massage time to visualize, and fall deep into a relaxing trance. This is a time when you can listen to your inner guidance and what it has to say. You intuition is very powerful, and when all the noise gets quiet, you will begin to hear your inner self. Your inner voice is always trying to guide you. Tune into it. Connect with it. Be patient and loving to yourself.

Apply affirmations to strengthen your mindset to believe in your goals. Spend five minutes looking in the mirror and speaking loving, encouraging words to yourself. This mirror technique will help you love yourself more and connect with the inner light and beauty that you are. Don't be afraid to look yourself in the eye, and tell yourself you are great and that you are good enough. When you nurture yourself, your inner light begins to glow. Your confidence and self-love will shine from the inside out, because you believe in yourself. This is a big part of the manifestation process, because it shows that you feel worthy of receiving what you ask for. When you own your greatness, great things begin to happen in your life.

I hope these five steps have provided you with some insight as to how you can start increasing your vibration right now, so you can become more harmonious with what you want to manifest. You have the choice to start implementing these changes at this very moment. *To know is one thing, but to do is where all the magic happens.* I hope this helps you reach the next level in your growth.

9

Spirit - You Are Beyond the Physical

Birth and death are the greatest reminders that we are beyond the physical. If you pay close attention, you'll notice that everything about you is beyond the physical. Your thoughts, imagination, and that which sustains you can't be seen. Knowing that you are beyond the physical is an empowering feeling that can help you learn to go with the flow instead of taking everything in life so seriously. Everything passes on. I always ask myself, "Where was I before I was born?" This profound question automatically connects me back to my spirit. You are beyond the physical, and the realities of death and leaving the physical body serve as a reminder that you are flowing, animated, and present in your human form right now. The more you remember who you truly are, the more you can snap out of earthly illusions and focus on living a more meaningful life filled with purpose.

Think about how easily you breathe without concerning yourself with your next breath. You can cultivate an underlying trust without worrying about how things work. You don't know how the sun will rise in the morning, but you trust that it will. Everything in life is miraculous. You have to put your attention and mind on how much the source of life endlessly gives and provides for us all. If you put your trust in this kind of power, you will never have to worry about how things will happen for you.

Miracles and unexpected blessings happen on a daily basis. Switch your mindset to the abundance that surrounds you. Take a moment to watch how precisely the universe functions without a single error. Look at the way the ocean flows. Look at the endlessness of the sky. Stare at the stars. Get out of your mind for once, and be present with the blessings that already surround you. To remember your spirit, you have to notice the everyday miracles that happen in the universe and in your life. An awareness of subtle energies allows you to notice the flow of things. When you remember your spirit, you will begin to awaken and recognize that you are a powerful being.

Everything you imagine, visualize, and think has the potential to be your reality. You have been creating your entire life up to this point. Nothing is by chance or a coincidence. The moments you have found challenging have only strengthened you. What was removed from your life served to teach you about the goodness you actually deserve. Every aspect of life is just. It is not about judging what is happening, but rather accepting what the lessons are, what they are teaching you, and what you can learn from the experience.

When you want to create your vision and manifest something, you have to learn to let it go and trust in the unseen to provide. As your manifestations are aligning, be in an energetic state of receiving. Do your mindset, habits, and behaviors match what you want to manifest? Do you feel like you are ready to let go and step up into a new frequency? It is all up to you to be prepared to receive. The universe will make the delivery, and during the time between the setting of your intention and the manifesta- tion of your goal, remain patient and keep believing. Trust that it is arriving as easily as your next breath.

Centering Yourself

Be at peace, and center your emotions so you can attract what you want. We all have the ability to manifest our reality. There's nothing stopping you from creating your experience. You do it every day with your mind. You see more of what you think about. You experience more of what you put your energy into. The point is to start doing it at will, and to get the best out of your mind's own power. Manifesting is believing in yourself and knowing that you can experience the reality you want. When you're in a high-energy state, you easily draw to yourself the experiences you want because you FEEL good. Emotions play a major role in the manifesting process.

The most important lesson I've learned in the process of manifesting is getting my feelings in check. Sometimes, we want certain things to happen in our lives, but we sabotage the manifestations with our emotions of fear, doubt, and lack of trust. These emotions will usually block our natural ability to receive. We're all in the flow. The more we learn to trust, let go, and be open to what can happen, the easier the process of manifesting becomes.

Our feelings are great indicators of what is going on internally that we need to check on. Thoughts usually trigger an emotion, and that emotion goes back to trigger more of the same thoughts. If you feel low, you have to start diving into your belief system, past experiences, and subconscious mind to discover what is causing the resistance. Once you identify the cause, you can change it by speaking, thinking, and feeling a new thought pattern.

The only difference between you and any other successful person (or someone with a great relationship, or someone who manifests their reality effortlessly) is where they're at with their emotions and beliefs. People who feel good in all circumstances usually have more power to believe that what they're going through at any given moment isn't their final destination. They have a vision in mind, and that's all they focus on. You have to learn how to stay positive and calm in all situations. Don't let your current circumstances make you believe that you can't have better. Your mindset is more important than what's happening. It's not always about being positive and having good vibes; it's not like life doesn't throw challenges and test your way. Things always happen. It is up to us to choose how we react and respond.

Reality is truly what you want it to be. Disconnect yourself from acting as an emotional button to external circumstances. Don't be swayed left or right. Be centered. Be at peace. Be hopeful. A believer is a visionary; they see in their mind's eye their true reality. They hold onto it until it happens. They are the true creators of their reality. Start manifesting and living the life you want by aligning your emotions with your visions. Be the one who decides how you want to feel. The more you master yourself, the better you become at creating what you want.

You must discipline your mind to avoid focusing on the how, why, and when. These are not matters you need concern yourself with; indeed, obsessing over these details can slow down manifestation. Do not doubt that your manifestations will happen. This can affect the universal balance and prevent your dreams from becoming a reality. You cannot simultaneously believe that something will happen and that it will not. The two types of thought will cancel each other out.

You cannot set positive intentions for yourself and do the opposite. The law of manifestation does not operate like this. It is vital, therefore, that in addition to clear, focused thoughts, your actions toward others, toward nature, and toward the universe are well-intentioned and wholesome. Ensure that your predominant qualities are kindness, compassion, respect, tolerance, happiness, gratefulness, understanding, and patience.

Start being grateful for everything in your life. When you're manifesting, you have no time for losing energy to ungratefulness and lack. Give out the beautiful energy you want to get back. The action part is being open to opportunities that show up, and taking steps to execute them. There will be a lot of signs on what to do, so be on the lookout.

As you are manifesting, make sure you're not being hard on yourself or taking things too seriously. The point of being here on earth is to enjoy life and remember that we are also creating our experiences. When you learn that you can do this, everything becomes fun. Be in a joyous spirit, and never take anything so personally that you become identified with it and allow it to limit your ability to do more. When you begin to master your own mind, you will know that all situations and circumstances depend upon your perception for a response. Everything is about how you decide to react to things. Be centered and easygoing so you can flow with the universe. You are a magical being. You are a powerful source. Everything starts with you.

Trusting the Unseen

I am sure you have been in situations in which something you wanted manifested unexpectedly. You probably have met someone who changed your life in the most unusual way. This is the power of trusting the unseen. When you want to manifest something, you have to start operating on a spiritual level. You can't expect to know exactly how something will happen. If you knew, you would probably limit yourself to a comfortable position. This is why the universe works in mysterious ways. You get aligned to people, opportunities, and great blessings in ways you can't predict. It just happens, and you're in the right place at the right time. This is the kind of power that is supporting you. This is the source that is with you, and has access to a greater vision. When you trust in it, you will see yourself succeeding and creating the life you want.

People who want to control how something happens limit themselves to what they already know. Your mind has to be able to flow with the universe in order to be able to receive unexpectedly. What the source wants to provide for you might be bigger and better than what you think you need and deserve. When you set your intention on manifesting, put it into the hands of the source. Let the alignments happen. Let yourself be surprised. When you trust in the unseen, you trust in your ability to manifest. Lose the feeling of having to obsess over how and when something will happen. Don't limit yourself. Believe in your greatest vision, and trust that the universe will assist you in manifesting it.

After you have put your manifestation out into the universe, start relaxing and being happy about it. Smile and be joyous. Do things that make you happy along the way. When you are in a happy state and you feel good about your manifestation, the universe pulls it toward you more quickly. Allow the universe to do its part while you are enjoying life. Believe that everything is on its way. How would you feel if you manifested what you wanted right now? Make that feeling of receiving your blessings more real for you. I always smile and say *thank you, universe, for blessing me* over and over again. Do this throughout the day. Thank the universe for providing for you and nurturing you. Be in a grateful state.

10

Welcome New Energy

The results you'll get from this book will change everything in your life. You are upgrading yourself and welcoming new energy. You are shifting your mindset and how you do things. You'll notice changes in your relationships, how you carry yourself, and the things you attract into your life. There will be new energy entering your life, since you are working on releasing old thought patterns, negative beliefs, and any limitations that once stood in your way. Your changes will inspire a whole new reality and way of handling things. You will become stronger and able to achieve more. You will not tolerate wasting your energy and time. You will start to prioritize what and who adds value to your life. Now that you have learned how important your mental energy is, you'll no longer be giving it away to negativity or people who used to drain you.

When You Shift, So Does Everything Else

Change starts with you. The people in your life and the situations you're experiencing are things you have attracted. You will only begin to appreciate this understanding when you finally see the kinds of people and opportunities you *can* attract. During the process of investing your energy into getting better, you'll notice that you begin to outgrow what doesn't help you evolve naturally.

I always say, don't force yourself to cut people off—just work on yourself. The frequency of the relationship will naturally shift, and you will no longer will be interested in continuing. New people will arrive. Be okay with letting go of the past and things that have become stagnant. If someone wants to change, they will change. Don't force yourself to make anyone grow. People who are ready to step it up will. Though it is exciting to share this wisdom with people and tell them that they are powerful and can create their own reality, most people will have to decide for themselves to do the inner work. It's great to know that you can change your reality and manifest what you want, but it's another thing to come face to face with thought patterns that no longer serve you. Inner work requires dedication, passion, and consistency. This is accepting that you are responsible for what you create in this life, and that you are ready to consciously attract what you want.

During your manifestation process, I want you to commit to your vision and to really clearing things out of your life. When you take care of your mental, physical, and spiritual self, you will notice great rewards and benefits. Be patient with yourself throughout this process. There will be a lot of energy shifts and an end to the old ways. You don't have to speak about it. Let your results speak for themselves. Be low-key, and invest that energy in your growth.

When you are manifesting, don't speak about it unless the person has high energy and they believe in themselves. Most people who don't believe in themselves will think what you're doing is odd, or they will try to discourage you. They will even tell you to be realistic.

What does "being realistic" mean, anyway? Life is proof enough that everything is magical and miraculous. You have an imagination for a reason. Never be discouraged by anyone who doesn't believe in you.

This is why I believe in letting your reality and the things you're creating speak for themselves. Be your own mastermind, and feed your visions with faith on a daily basis. For so many years, people have talked down to others with great ideas, only because they didn't think something was possible. What others think has nothing to do with "reality." You decide what is real for you. You decide what you can visualize and create. Nobody can do that for you. Keep things to yourself until they manifest. Only share your manifestation goals with someone who is very positive, happy, and supportive. These kinds of people will help you with your vision by further encouraging you and keeping you focused.

If the people who doubt you or bring negativity are family members, don't allow yourself to take what they say personally. The more you stop energetically resisting or pushing them away, the less they will bother you. Just smile, and know that everything you're working on is happening on the mental plane and getting ready to manifest into the physical. Pray for those who doubt you. They need it the most, because they have failed to know what the power of the mind and imagination can create for those who believe in what is possible. Simply send love to them mentally, even when they try to push their negativity on you.

Don't forget, your inner reality belongs to you. Nothing anyone says or does can come through and stay without your permission. Don't give anyone power over you. Let people think and say what they want. Just stay positive, and love those who are hard to love. You are too busy to be distracted from your goals. Keep your frequency high. Stay centered and calm during challenging situations, especially when you feel a lot of doubt or fear. Step back and away from everything and read your manifestation journal. You have visions to manifest; you don't have time to entertain negativity or doubt.

During your manifestation process, remove yourself from toxic environments and situations that lower your vibrations. Don't worry about what falls apart during this time. Keep your mind focused on what you're grateful for and what is coming. When you ask for something better, new space needs to be created for a fresh start. Be okay with what exits, and be welcoming to what enters. Make a conscious effort to change and move into something bigger and better. When you start upgrading your mindset, new energy will enter your life. Be ready to receive, because it is on the way.

11

Manifest Now Technique

- Seven-Day Speed Manifestation -

First and foremost, I'd like to give you a little warning that this technique will literally help you manifest what you want extremely quickly. When I first did it for seven days, I started receiving what I wanted within two days. I was initially blown away by it, and it even made me sit for a moment in awe of the vast powers to which we have access. I noticed that the universe responds right away when you speak, think, and feel things in urgency. When there is a high level of focus and clear feelings and thoughts invested in the results, everything starts to happen right away.

The Manifest Now technique is about receiving now. It's about owning the state and feeling the results now. When we harness our internal state in this moment to manifest what we want, we receive it more quickly. If we say *three months from now* or *one year from now*, we don't hold the same intensity on the vision and goal we want to receive right away. Of course, you can have long-term goals, but this is all about manifesting now. Live, feel, think, and believe in what you want to manifest right now.

When you apply the Manifest Now technique, you'll notice instant results happening right away. You'll probably notice them in the same hour or the same day. It is that powerful. I have seen miraculous results happen in seven days. Always remember that you are a powerful being. Once you make a command and speak something into the universe, the alignment begins to happen right away.

Here is what you'll do in this technique for the next seven days.

1. Write down what you want to manifest quickly (in the next seven days or less) in your manifestation journal as if it has already happened: "I manifested _____, and I am so HAPPY!" Write this statement down 100 times. If you have multiple things you want to manifest, do the same thing, and write it 100 times. Repetition and your own handwriting are powerful, and this technique shows intensity, focus, and determination. You are also writing down the results and feeling happy about it as if it has already happened for you. Read what you wrote 100 times, and feel the emotion and excitement behind the words. Repeat the writing part once a day for seven days, and read the whole thing three times a day with happiness and joy.

2. Every morning when you wake up, say to yourself, "I am receiving good news in the next 24 hours." Take it a step further, and write it down in your manifestation journal. Let these words become a part of your daily routine. This is a powerful, energizing statement that begins to attract everything to you right away. I remember doing this for so long, and every single day, I kept receiving good news. It has never failed me. I believe the power of this tech-

nique has to do with the fact that you know that something great is about to Manifest Now. Not in one day. Not in the distant future. Right now, in this moment—when we think, feel, and connect with everything.

Once we speak such powerful words, we begin to notice what is good in our lives. Your brain and the universe team up to help you be on the lookout for what is right. In this state of feeling good and expecting good, you also start to relax and trust the universe. This is where the magic happens. We surrender because we know that in the next 24 hours, good news is on the way. When we project our manifestations into the future, we start to doubt and overthink. This daily reminder that you speak for yourself will start to awaken your mind and activate your full ability to manifest swiftly. People I have shared this with have sometimes seen results in as little as 20 minutes. The universe works outside of space and time. We limit the experience of receiving when we start to put so much emphasis on the future instead of this moment. Now is all you have. Believe within you, right now, that you will receive good news in the next 24 hours.

3. Repeat "Thank you, universe, for giving me _____! I am so grateful!" This is a powerful statement, because you are already happy and excited for what you are going to receive. This gratitude also shows that you trust and believe in what is about to happen for you. Gratitude raises your frequency and puts you in receiving mode.

4. In the morning, when you wake up, spend 15 minutes visualizing what you want to happen. See

the image as clearly as possible. Smile as you watch the vision of you receiving what you are focused on manifesting. Invoke a feeling of happiness and excitement with the vision. Repeat the visualization again before bedtime. Let that be the last thing you think about before falling asleep. If you have more time, do 30 minutes in the morning and 30 minutes at night. The more time you invest, the clearer the vision and end goal will become in your mind's eye. However, even 15 minutes is a very powerful force that will instantly create alignment and make a delivery on your manifestations.

5. Start sending love to what you want to receive. Love is the highest frequency, and can influence your attraction level toward what you want to welcome into your life. This is a miraculous technique, because you are going above any mental chatter or ideas about how and when things will happen. Instead, you are welcoming it by being thankful for it. Always know that what you want also wants you. There is no reason you can't have what your heart desires. Send love out, and know that all is okay. Everything you think, feel, and speak for your highest good is coming toward you now. Be filled with so much joy and happiness, as your manifestation is arriving any second now.

6. Answer these six questions in your manifestation journal, and read them daily for the next seven days.

- What would you be doing right now if you manifested what you wanted?
- How would you feel?
- What would your life be like?
- Who would you share all your blessings with?

- Who would be the first person you shared your good news with?
- How would they look, sound, and feel about your manifestation?

The goal of these questions is to help you feel the emotion and step into the reality of what it would be like for you to have exactly what you want. Remember, the more feelings and visualizations you attach to the answers, the quicker you'll see results. Manifesting is about owning the frequency of what you want right now.

7. For the next seven days, do some kind of physical activity that works best for you, and repeat your manifestation affirmations during your workout. Since your body is releasing serotonin during your workout, you can connect your words to that state, and your body and mind will be very alert to absorb it all in. One thing I did during my seven days was to take a walk next to the ocean for 30 minutes and repeat my affirmations. I kept saying, "I am thankful for what I have manifested." I smiled and felt so good the whole time. I felt at peace with everything, and trusted that the universe was working for me.

8. If you are trying to manifest a financial break-through, incorporate the Magnetic Money Mindset technique in Section Fourteen.

9. Have fun! Do everything that makes you feel good during the next seven days. Don't sit around and worry about when your manifestation will arrive. The whole point is to trust that it is already here. This frequency shifts everything toward you, because you believe that what you want already

belongs to you. I remember when my manifestation arrived, I was out celebrating myself. Yes—I committed a whole day to treating myself at a spa, had dinner, and socialized. I lived life, and kept a high frequency that all was well and all was good. I got a call about what I was expecting, and just like that, everything fell into place. Trust that the universe will deliver, and go enjoy your life. Spend time with your loved ones. Do anything and everything that makes you feel alive.

Apply this technique, and watch unexpected miracles unfold in your life.

12

Release It

10 Powerful Techniques You Can Use on a Daily Basis to Release Any Mental, Physical, or Emotional Blocks That Hinder Your Manifesting Powers

The fastest way to manifest and create a space of welcoming new energy into your life is to let go of the old. You have to know how to release things out of your life so you can welcome new energy, new people, new experiences, and new opportunities. This section will teach you 10 powerful techniques you can start applying to your life on a daily basis to get on the manifesting wave.

Most of what holds us back from getting what we want is the fear of letting go of what we have in our lives, even when it is no longer working. At any given time, you have the ability to release yourself from anything that hinders you. The ability to release and cleanse your energy and environment is up to you. You can't ask for something new and expect to stay the same. Everything in your life will change once you declare that you are ready to release all that is holding you back from being your greatest self. Within you right now lies all the potential to be centered, at peace, and in love with the life you're living. You have the power right now to tap into the deepest part of your soul and feel the endless universal love surrounding you. You are not alone. You are not left behind. You are exactly where you are, and the ability to change that is the discovery you're making at this moment to completely turn your life around.

The power to release things is the gift of surrendering to the universe, and it is also the highest form of trust that something greater can come into your life. Nothing in this world is ever lost. We let go, only to gain. We remove, only to welcome. This is a never-ending process, and as we evolve, we are challenged to step up and move into a higher frequency. The baggage of the past must be given up. You have to start the surrendering process so you can cultivate faith in what's to come.

Learning to release will strengthen your ability to manifest. You will feel lighter, happier, and more excited to make room for new energy to enter your life. The universe will start to provide, filling the cleared spaces with the energy your heart and mind desire. Instead of giving your energy away to the past, you are now channeling it toward your visions. Each time you release it, you are also freeing your mental and emotional energy to do better. You are taking all that free energy and directing it toward your dreams. From this day on, you will no longer waste your precious life force on things that drain you. You have discovered the power to release them, and harness your energy for living your best life.

Below, I will give you some of the most powerful techniques to release anything that's blocking you from manifesting your dreams. I highly recommend that you use one technique per day, so you can work through each step to truly maximize your abilities. The more you apply yourself, the greater the results will be. Take it one day at a time as you begin to release, let go, and welcome energy.

Day 1

- Clear Your Energy -

Clearing your energy is so crucial to the process of releasing what doesn't belong in your life. Your mind and body are always picking up on energy from the environment, other people, and situations that you experience throughout the day. When something we don't like happens, we tend to feel that energy in our gut, and sometimes, it stays on our mind longer than it should. This step is going to help you begin the clearing process so you no longer have to ponder negative, limiting, or draining energy.

The first step in clearing your energy is knowing that when something doesn't feel right, or you feel a sense of heaviness, you can quickly release it through conscious awareness. I am teaching you that you can clear your energy through your mind. You don't have to use any tools or products. Simply create a vision in your mind in which you see a waterfall cleansing you of any negative, low-vibrational, or draining energy. The waterfall technique is similar to taking a shower and washing all the negative energy away. You can use this technique anytime and anywhere. Simply switch on the waterfall over your head to cleanse your energy and help release what doesn't belong in your mind or body. When you feel any unusual energy, always activate this technique to cleanse your mind and emotions.

Visualization is a powerful tool when you are learning how to work with your own imaginative abilities. As with physical goals, you can use mental images and scenarios to get your desired outcome. You have the ability within you, at this moment, to clear your energy using your imagination. Throughout the 10 techniques, I will be guiding you through steps that allow you to fully create mental/visual experiences that will help you release any thought patterns, emotions, or negative energy that don't serve you or help you reach your ultimate goal.

- Waterfall Technique -

I chose a waterfall as a visualization technique to clear your energy because waterfalls are known to have the highest levels of negative ions, which enhance mood and improve overall mental, physical, and spiritual wellness. Nature is thriving on the same healing negative ions that clear out your energy, allowing you to be renewed and cleansed at any moment.

Applying the Technique

When applying this technique, simply visualize a never-ending rush of water falling over the top of your head and all the way to the ground. Feel it cleansing, clearing, and releasing any energies that don't belong in your body. Just as you take a shower to clean your body, feel the same renewing energy as you use the waterfall technique. This is one of my favorites, because it is easy to visualize and feel the change right away.

Day 2

- Mental Vacuum Technique -

The mental vacuum technique is something I have been using for a while, and it will help you suck out any thoughts you don't want in your mind. The technique is basically imagining a vacuum over any thought you don't want, switching it on, and watching it get sucked away. The other side of the vacuum is oblivion. Once that thought is pulled out of your mind, it is gone forever. This is a powerful tool to use to clear out negative, draining thoughts. The mental vacuum is at your fingertips to activate anytime a thought you don't want comes to mind.

During your manifestation process, old thought patterns and negative thinking could come back to test you or challenge your new positive mindset. The point isn't to ignore them; the goal is to get rid of them completely. Using mental techniques like these will give you an extra tool to visualize, feel, and release what doesn't belong in your mental space. During this time, you will be cultivating new ideas, thought patterns, and positive thoughts so you can manifest more efficiently. Access to this mental vacuum is a great means of releasing and letting go of what doesn't belong in your mental headspace.

Applying the Technique

When a negative thought comes into your mind, imagine a huge vacuum over the thought, and visualize it getting sucked out of your thought pattern. When the thought disappears into oblivion, invoke a feeling of happiness. Smile, and feel good that you were able to finally release that negative thought. Be sure to use this technique when doubt, worry, or fear come into your mind as you are transforming and manifesting. The more you release the thoughts that don't belong there, the more you make room for healthier, more productive ones to enter.

Day 3

- Golden Light Technique -

Gold light is a very high frequency that can be used to assist your mind, body, and soul to let go and become charged with high-frequency manifesting energy. We are all connected to the word *light*, and associate it with goodness, clarity, peace, and positivity. Golden light has an extra, extremely powerful energy that can assist you in reaching any state you like. Each night, before you go to bed, visualize golden energy vibrating very highly. This light carries a frequency that lets you release, clear, and let go of any negative energy held within your body. The golden light not only clears your energy, but also charges your body with the highest frequency so you can manifest what you want. When you are vibrating highly and you have released any emotional blocks within your body, the possibilities become endless. I also recommend using this technique before visualizing, so you can charge your energy to manifest and create what you want.

Applying the Technique

First, relax your body, and take five deep breaths. Once you are relaxed, watch a golden light of peace, love, happiness, calm, and positive energy enter your body, from the top of your head all the way to your feet. With each movement of the light, feel your body letting go of any emotional blocks, and feel a sense of peace coming over you. This high-frequency golden light can clear away any blocks and help you get charged up to pull in your manifestations. This golden light can be accessed anywhere, at any time. Simply feel its presence recharging your entire body and helping you release any pain, doubt, discomfort, or negative energy.

Day 4

- Cutting Cords with the Past -

If you feel like you are stuck in the past or attached to someone from another time in your life, this technique will help free your energy from what is no longer present. Understand that the past is gone. No matter what someone has done to you or what happened to you before, in this moment, all of that is done. Now we have to free your mental energy from past attachments so you can use that energy to create what you want today.

If someone has hurt you, or you have regrets from the past, you have to be prepared to cut the cord connecting you to that experience. Free your emotions and thoughts from that connection. Release yourself from the cycle of could have, should have and would have. When you are making these powerful changes to manifest the reality you want, you must be willing to let go. The cord is basically what keeps your mental and emotional energy stuck on someone or something that's no longer in your life. If you keep having repetitive thoughts about people who once did you wrong or broke your heart, then you are giving that person or situation energy through an invisible cord, which keeps you attached and depletes your energy. Today is the day to cut the cord. It is time to move forward with your life and make peace with the past.

Applying the Technique

If there is someone or something from the past con-stantly taking your energy, imagine them in front of you, and see a cord between yourself and the person. Let yourself feel the energy of peace and love toward that person as you cut the cord between the two of you. The energy of peace and love is what is going to free you and help you to let go. Forgive them and smile. Wave goodbye to them, and see them peacefully disappearing into thin air. Once the cord is cut, none of your energy will ever go to them again. You have finally freed yourself to use your mental and emotional energy toward creating your own reality and being at peace. Use this technique to disconnect from the past whenever you find yourself being drained or pulled back to it. You must sever the cord and release that old connection.

Day 5

- Welcoming New Energy -

Since you are working on welcoming a lot of new energy into your life, the most important step that will assist you in the process is clearing your life, space, and energy state from any noise/clutter. When you are ready for change, you must also be ready to receive what the universe is about to bring into your life. The first step is getting rid of anything in your life that isn't working for you. Start by clearing your home space from excess items that you no longer have a need for. Get rid of things with bad memories attached to them. Commit to making everything around you lighter. When you clear your physical space of old things and old memories, you are preparing for more exciting things to enter.

Another way to welcome new energy is to make peace with letting go of people who drain your energy. This is a time for you to make great changes in your life. The more you apply the tools and wisdom, the greater success and results you'll receive. There can no longer be any excuses for keeping anyone or anything around that tries to keep you stuck in old energy patterns. Rest assured that the welcoming of new energy is a tool that is available to you each time you let go of something. Believe that something bigger and better is on the way for you.

Applying the Technique

Clear your space in your home.
Clear your mental space from old connections.
Clear and let go of people who bring any negativity into
your life.

Day 6

- Forgive Right Away -

Forgiving frees you from being emotionally and mentally drained by someone or something that no longer matters. Whatever has happened has happened. To carry the pain and memories around can only weigh heavily on you and make you feel hurt and sad as a result of something that no longer exists. During this transformative time, I want you to start mentally and emotionally making peace with the past or the people who have hurt you. Forgive them for the pain they have caused you. This is something you do mentally and emotionally. Holding grudges and living in the past takes up way too much of your energy. Wouldn't you want to move forward?

My favorite thing to do now is to forgive right away. I don't hold onto anything from the past, or even from yesterday. Forgiving others saves your energy. You don't have to go back to them or deal with any of their negativity. You can just forgive to free yourself from the attachment. The goal is to start every day fresh and feeling good about yourself. You are a powerful being, and your mind, body, and soul should be focused on the life you want to create, not what has happened to you. This is a perfect time to make peace with those who have done you wrong. Forgive and move on with your life.

Applying the Technique

Forgive yourself every night before going to bed for anything you feel like you've done wrong that day. This is the perfect time to let go and enter your sleep so you can wake up fresh and new the next morning.

Forgive others by mentally releasing the grudges, regrets, and pain they have caused you. Watch all of that being lifted off of you. Speak in your mind and heart that you are ready to forgive that person, and that you wish them peace and love.

Day 7

- Nobody Can Drain You -

This is kind of an advanced technique, because it gives you back your power to be in charge of where you get your energy and whom you share it with. When I say nobody can drain you, I mean just that. I have learned that I can tap into the unlimited source that provides me energy on a consistent basis, without needing it from others.

Imagine that you have an unlimited supply of energy pouring into you every day. This is the energy you have access to. Nobody can deplete it, or take it away from you. Even when you encounter negative people or a negative situation, don't personalize what they are saying or doing. Just observe, but don't absorb. Most people personalize what other people think, and feel drained by their words. Nobody has the power over you to cause you to lose energy. You get to decide, right in this moment, that nobody can drain you—and that you have access to an unlimited supply of universal energy.

Applying the Technique

Every day, feel that you have large amounts of unlimited universal energy being poured into your life. This supply is unlimited, and you have access to it right now. Just being aware of it will fill you up with so much energy. The next time you are in what might seem like a draining situation, feel a sudden rush of universal energy being poured into you, from the top of your head all the way down to your feet. This is what will keep you nourished— not anything or anyone outside of yourself. Tap in.

Day 8

- Just Breathe Through It -

Anytime you are faced with a challenging situation, just breathe through it. Breathing deeply actually slows down your brainwaves from overthinking so you can relax, and the more you do it, the better you will become at remaining calm during difficult situations. During this transformational time, you might deal with situations that test your patience. I want you to remember to breathe before you overreact, respond, or regret what you might say. When you step back and breathe through difficult situations, you open yourself up to be more centered so you can find solutions. Always make decisions when you are calm and relaxed.

Applying the Technique

When you feel like you are overthinking or stressing out, just take a deep breath and let it go. Do this 10-15 times until you feel relaxed. After each breath, remind yourself that everything will work out for you. This is a moment to remember your goals and dreams. Don't let anything get in the way of your manifestations, not even small temporary emotions.

Day 9

- No Identity -

Don't identify with pain. Don't identify with past mistakes, or even current mistakes. Your soul is beyond the physical, and all the labels you put on yourself only limit you from being greater and better than any circumstance. Just be. Don't attach yourself to anything. Life is momentary, and all the experiences we are having are temporary. Why not make the best memories and be free?

No matter what is happening in your life right now, it does not define you. Who you are is limitless and beyond the physical. If you look back, you'll see that you have changed, grown, and recreated yourself so many times. You might even look back and laugh at certain things you used to do. This is the power of your soul observing physical experiences. You keep evolving. Nothing can define who you are and who you can become. This is what keeps you going. Start using this wisdom in your life when you find yourself putting labels and definitions on yourself. Remind yourself that you are unlimited and beyond the physical. You can change and recreate yourself anytime. Don't let anyone keep you in a box—not even yourself.

Applying the Technique

Repeat daily:

I am not my past.
I am not my mistakes.
I am limitless, and beyond the physical.
I can recreate myself and renew my mindset on a daily basis.

Take a moment, and observe how often you label yourself. Are these labels helping you get better? Are you expanding, or staying stuck? Never tell yourself *that's just who I am.* You can change, and this is an opportunity to be honest and real with yourself so you can let go of all the identities, labels, and limitations.

Day 10

- Live in the Moment -

Every time you see your mind going into the past or future, snap out of it and bring yourself back to this moment. This moment right now is the only time you have to fully create your past and design your future. What you do today will determine how you live in the future and what your past will look like. If you give your energy to the power of now, then you will be able to stop wasting your energy on the past and do something about your life today. During the manifestation process, your mind will try to take you back to the past to make you doubt what you can do today. You need to remember that each moment is brand new, and today is the day you WILL change your life.

Applying the Technique

If your mind keeps going into the past, bring it back to now. Tell yourself: *I am in a new day and a new energy. I will not go back to the past to live there—I will only use past experience as motivation to keep moving forward.* If you keep worrying about the future, always bring yourself back to this moment by telling yourself: *I am creating my future now.* Always maximize your day so you can create a beautiful past and a fruitful future by applying the power of now.

13

Think It

35 Powerful Thoughts to Keep You Energized, Focused, and Excited to Manifest

Read these words daily to keep your frequency high so you can manifest quickly.

Your thoughts are powerful. I have put together 35 powerful, energetically-charged phrases that will help you stay focused, inspired, motivated, and excited to manifest. This is a collection of my most inspirational thoughts that helped me during my own manifestation process. There were days when I needed extra motivation, and I would read these words to keep me going. You, too, can **think it** and be inspired.

Every single day, I want you to read these 35 thoughts and feel the energy behind them. Use the words to keep your frequency high and excited to manifest what you want. I believe the words to which we expose ourselves have a powerful impact on our mindset. This is why the books you read completely alter how you think. I have hand-selected words that will help you feel the energy of abundance, love, freedom, and possibility.

Charge yourself daily with these 35 thoughts, and think of them throughout the day as a reminder to stay encouraged.

1. Good news is on the way.

Repeat daily:

Good things are coming my way.
Good things are coming my way.
Good things are coming my way.
Good things are coming my way.

So many great things are coming your way. Don't be afraid of new beginnings. If you're going over a bump in the road or feel unsure, don't worry. You're on the right track. As with any great change, a shedding of the "old ways" is required. Anytime we're in a transformative state, we get kind of uncomfortable, because we're not use to it. Sometimes, we even desire to go back to old habits, just to avoid this feeling. I'm here to tell you not to be afraid.

Don't shy away. Don't hide from it. Allow change to flow through your life. As you become more aware, you'll begin to take conscious control of your life. You'll no longer be a victim of circumstance, but rather the creator of your reality. Everything in your life is about to change. Be a little more patient, and trust the process.

If you didn't already know, there's an important universal law called the Law of Gestation. This law basically means that there is a natural process and order to things once they have been planted. The Law of Gestation works in nature: growing trees and crops, and even in all reproductive systems. The truth is right in front of our faces, even if we don't pay attention. This is why we have to learn to respect and honor the process.

We must believe that something greater can happen and learn to immerse ourselves in patience even when we don't see the signs right away. Our hidden superpower that unlocks miracles is found within patience and faith. Keep believing that good things are on the way.

2. Believe in it until it becomes your reality.

Repeat daily:

My mind is powerful.
I can manifest what I want.
I see the vision clearly.
It is happening now.

Ever since I discovered the power of my thoughts, my life hasn't been the same. Just like everyone else, I used to think my reality was out of my control. I used to think that certain situations happening to me were "predestined," when in reality, I was creating my destiny through my thoughts. I just didn't know! This was my greatest discovery when I started studying my mind, habits, beliefs, and the kinds of thoughts I was entertaining. Doing the inner work is so rewarding. Choose to become aware so you can break free of unconscious creations of situations and circumstances you don't want to be in.

Realization

The first thing you need to understand is that EVERYTHING in the world begins and happens as a result of the power of thoughts. Everything around you was once a thought. The thoughts you choose, combined with your emotions, will mold and shape your life physically, financially, relationally, emotionally, and spiritually.

The Reality of Things

Because we get so occupied with external reality, we don't really give much focus to internal reality, which is where creation originates. Everything outside of yourself has already been created. So, if you're experiencing it now, it's basically a thought that has already manifested. However, there are unlimited possibilities for where you can be, who you can become, and what you can do with your life. At this moment, anything is possible for you. If you choose to believe what your five senses are telling you, then you're only going to recreate what has already been created. If you consciously decide to go into your imagination and choose to experience something different, then you can rewrite your story.

There's No Limit

You can't limit yourself any longer. Life is full of possibilities, and all it takes is going inside and changing your thoughts to the ones you want to experience. Forget what outside reality appears to be telling you. Focus on where you want to be in your imagination. Visualize it like you're living it. Walk around as if you're there. Nothing can stop you when you discover your power.

3. Don't worry about how things are going to work out; just believe that they will.

Repeat daily:

Today, I surrender to the universe to guide me.
I trust that the universe will provide the way.
Everything is working out for me.
Thank you, universe, for blessing me today.

Never worry, stress, or overthink how everything you're going to manifest or receive will happen for you. Just believe that it will. Believe in it. Feel the energy of your manifestation arriving. There's great power in believing what you can envision in your mind, rather than accept what's happening in front of you.

Everything that can happen for you starts with a single thought. You have to believe in it until it shows up. The more you believe in that thought, the more you will feel it. The more you feel it, the more quickly it will manifest into your reality. Trust in the greater power that's constantly aligning everything for you through your visions and inner state of being. Choose to connect with your higher power to guide you through this process of change and receiving. You will grow stronger every day, because you trust the energy that sustains you. How can you not trust the source that powers all of life so precisely without a single error?

Don't let fear, negativity, or lower-vibrational energy steal your shine. Noticing blessings is just a matter of perspective. See the light in every situation. See what's coming to an end as a new beginning. Learn to observe without getting caught up in everything. Feel the subtle energies that are guiding you. See what's moving everything and what's giving it so much life. Connect with it. Connect with your spirit during this time of great transformation. You'll be blessed for life.

4. Don't let the process between the time you declare what you want to manifest and the moment it comes into your reality make you panic or worry if it's actually going to happen. You must trust, believe, and have unwavering faith that what you intend will manifest.

Repeat daily:

I will be patient today.
I believe in my ability to manifest.
The things I want to manifest are on the way.
I am feeling stronger and more trusting of the universe.

I'm going to keep speaking great things into existence for my life. I know how powerful my mind is. I know the power of my words and what I believe in. I'm going to start attracting everything I want, by becoming what I ask for. Change starts with me. If I am not happy, I have to do something about it. I know that I am not my past. I am not my mistakes. Starting today, I'll stop telling that old story and recreate myself. I will remain focused on my goals. Even if I have a moment of difficulty, I will not give up. I know success comes with consistency. I know that I will make it. I will get better.

No problem or challenge will stop me. I just have to believe, with the power of my mind, that what I think, feel, and focus upon will manifest for me. What I'm looking for is inside of me. I'm going to align with my spirit and trust the wisdom I receive. I'm ready to be blessed. I know happiness, love, and peace are an inside job. I'm going to start taking responsibility for my life. I'll start switching my thoughts and words to focus on what I want. I believe that I will manifest my greatest dreams. Nothing and nobody can get in the way of what's meant for me. I just have to be patient and trust the process.

I have to allow instead of stressing out. It will all work out for me. Everything I deserve is flowing toward me easily and effortlessly. Everything is energy aligning with itself. I'm being aligned to my greatest purpose. I'm going to be kind and patient with myself during the process of manifesting my visions. I believe in myself.

5. Stay calm in all situations.

Repeat daily:

I can get through anything.
I will stay calm and believe.
I got this.
My focus is on my vision.

No matter what's happening, just be calm about it. Everything will be okay. Stop overthinking it. One of the major setbacks we experience is being stuck somewhere mentally when we're no longer there physically. Constantly repeating scenarios from the past only hinders us from finding the real solutions and inner peace that we could be experiencing today.

That Old Thing

When we try to hold onto people and situations from the past, we limit our growth and prevent new energy from entering our lives. Think about this. You were okay before you met that person; you were fine before that thing happened to you. So why do you think you can't live without them now? Well, the thing about our minds is, once we experience something, our energy tunes into it. It can easily consume us if we're not aware that we are capable of redirecting our thoughts. What most people don't realize is that thoughts have the ability to reconnect, recreate, and re-energize us to tune into the present rather than being driven crazy by the past.

Newness

As creatures of habit, we limit ourselves to the small scope of reality we know, when in fact, our potential is endless. Each time you choose to be stuck in the past or allow your inner peace to be shaken, you lose potential energy you could be using to make a change in your life today. Once we free our energy from going toward negative thoughts, fear, or the past, we become open to new experiences and lose the idea of attachment. Life is meant to flow freely, so be open to change constantly.

It's your time.

It's time to get back in tune with yourself. Your mind, thoughts, and feelings all belong to you. You choose every single day where you want to direct them. It's unfortunate that most people choose to pour all that precious energy into their past, not realizing how much life has to offer in the moment. Taking back your power means being aware of where you stand in this vast universe. Know that you're not defined by one mistake, you're not who you were, and you're not what people think about you. Stop limiting yourself. Take back control. You deserve to be free.

6. To attract better, you have to become better yourself.

Repeat daily:

Everything starts with me.
I have the power to change today.
I take responsibility for my life.
Great blessings are headed my way.

The quickest way to take back your power and gain full control over your life is to take responsibility for the things you've attracted. Instead of blaming others or pointing fingers, ask yourself what lesson this situation or circumstance is here to teach you. Since energy is everything, nothing is a coincidence. Your thoughts, emotions, and beliefs are sent out to the environment to attract to yourself what you think and feel. When a situation presents itself and you're not happy with it, you don't have to blame what's happening. Rather, bless where you're at by being thankful for what it has taught you, and be open to ways you can evolve from it. This will automatically empower you to attract better experiences, because you're not a victim. Everything around you is energy.

The alignment you attract in the physical is a match for your mental/inner reality. If you don't like what you've attracted up to this point, release the circumstances. They are just results of your thinking. You should never blame anyone or anything for what you've attracted; that just weakens your personal power to take responsibility for your life.

Instead, focus back on the thoughts, beliefs, and ideas you have about the world. What is that little voice in your head constantly saying? What emotion are you always holding? Your state of being is constantly gravitating everything toward you. You can't keep asking for a particular relationship and hold a negative view on love. You can't keep asking for financial freedom and hold a negative view on money.

It's not what we say we "want," but the belief we have about it. Everyone desires change, but to become better, you have to start doing the self-work by owning your life. You start by letting go of all the resentments from the past and what went wrong. Once you become detached from the noise and own your power, you have the opportunity to increase your vibration to attract the experience you want. The better you become, the better you attract. Everything starts with you!

7. I am physically, mentally, and emotionally ready to enter a new phase in my life. I'm ready to grow and get better. I want to be the best me.

Repeat daily:

I am ready to change.
I welcome new energy.
It is time for me to step it up.
I am investing in myself today.

It's time to step everything up. There's absolutely no excuse for not being the best version of yourself. Elevate! Put your energy and time into what makes you happy. There's nothing more important than prioritizing your mind, body, and spirit. When you learn to love yourself, you'll start to leave behind things that are unhealthy for you. That means people, beliefs, and habits—anything that keeps you small.

Get Better

Your time is precious. Don't waste it on people who don't see the value in you, and never wait for others to see your value in order to value yourself. Every moment of your life is a chance to get better, find your purpose, and connect with the source that empowers you. Don't be distracted from it.

Know Your Worth

Don't wait for others to validate you or agree with how you choose to live your life. That's just a waste of time. Who cares, anyway? Just detach yourself. Take back your energy. It belongs to you!

Drama-Free

Don't involve yourself in drama and negativity. There's nothing that depletes your creativity more than meaningless bickering and useless conversations about others. So much is destroyed and lost when we use our energy in this manner. Let's go past that stage. Let's vibrate higher. Let's use our energy to heal, not hurt.

Elevate Yourself

A lot of people are aimless in their purpose, have no real plans, and are too occupied to evolve. Don't get sidetracked by these people. Own yourself and own your truth. Personal empowerment comes from standing up for what you believe in, even if you stand alone.

Be Determined

The more your vibration increases, the less you'll want to do what you used to do. You'll no longer care what anyone thinks of you. You'll suddenly find yourself craving life, living fully, loving deeply, and being so attentive to everything that fulfills you and makes you happy.

8. Be grateful that certain things didn't work out. Sometimes, you don't even know what you're being protected from, or where you're being guided when you're in the midst of it. That's why you just have to trust that greater things are aligning for you. Let go gracefully.

Repeat daily:

Everything that happens to me is happening for me.
I trust that what the universe needs to remove out of my life is for my highest good.
Greater blessings are aligning for me right now.
I am being guided to what I deserve.

Don't panic if you're being challenged, tested, or pushed right now. You might be going through a lot of transformation in your life that causes your limiting thoughts, negative activities/behaviors, and old ways of doing things to be challenged. You're starting to face yourself even more, and deal with the core of who you truly are by questioning everything you've been taught to believe. You're starting to notice yourself growing more, and no longer settling. You want more out of your journey. You want more out of life. You want to be real about who you are. You want to truly feel and really understand yourself.

A lot could be on your mind about your true purpose, and that's a great place to be. In the midst of taking the inner journey, your outer reality goes through some major shifts. Shifts that are pushing you toward an authentic life don't have room for low-vibrational energies that keep you stagnant or blind to your true potential. You start to disconnect from old friendships, relationships, and things that aren't fulfilling your soul. You might even start aligning with people and situations that fit your life beautifully. You find yourself getting stronger and less caught up. Some might even find themselves challenged by the shift, because they want to remain the same or stay in the same cycles.

Most pain comes from resisting growth and trying to hold on. Yes, the familiar always seems comfortable—but it's on the journey into the unknown that you discover your soul. In order to understand yourself, you have to know what you're made of. Don't try to avoid changes. Don't avoid growth. You have to fully allow the light to guide you on your journey by surrendering instead of resisting. Once we let go and allow instead of thinking we have all the answers, we suddenly find that everything makes sense. Trying so hard to force things can be the reason everything is stagnant in your life. Just breathe, and allow the shift to happen. Now is the time to start embracing your shift. Be open to what can enter by releasing what's holding you back.

9. Don't chase people to prove you matter. The energy of desperation repels people and makes them run further away. Love yourself, and glow up.

Repeat daily:

I let go of what needs to go.
I love myself.
I accept myself.
I am worthy.

Never chase anyone. The right people who belong in your life will come to you, and stay without force. The only thing you need to do right now is focus on bettering yourself. When you're not growing as a person, you will try to hold onto what's familiar, even when it's unhealthy for you. You don't have to be hurting, wondering, overthinking, and living in confusion when all it takes is turning your attention back to your own growth.

The Start of Change

When your soul is awakening to its truth, you'll go through a shift. So many changes will occur in your life. If you don't accept the changes and trust that it's time to evolve from things that aren't growing you, you'll experience problems. This is where the chasing and forcing occurs, because people are scared to grow into themselves. They get scared of the unknown and scared to let go, because the familiar is too comforting, even though it hurts them. The good news is that we need change. It pushes us out of our comfort zone and helps us grow. Even though there might be pain and discomfort during the process, it's definitely worth it in the end.

The Process of Change

Once you get to the point where you're done chasing, forcing, and trying to keep your past together, a beautiful thing happens: something called surrender. You let go and allow change to happen in your life. You're no longer focused on things outside of yourself to fulfill you. You go within to discover your inner strengths, beauty, light, and everything about you that'll elevate your life to new heights.

The Result

After you've shifted internally and changed as a person, your life will be much different. Now that you love yourself and feel whole within, the way you attract others to yourself will be completely different. You'll no longer be sending insecure signals, but rather the energy of strength, awareness, love, and kindness. This kind of energy will attract people on a similar path of self-discovery—people who respect and admire your light, and know how to walk by your side without force.

10. You're about to overcome something you've been dealing with. Your mind and heart will soon be at peace again. The weight is being lifted off of you right now. Breathe. Be patient. Everything will be okay.

Repeat daily:

I have the strength to get through anything.
I am strong enough.
I will keep going no matter what.
I have it in me to be the best I can be.

Right now, you might be in a situation that makes you think you won't survive, but six months ago, you were in a situation you didn't think you would survive, and two years before that, you were in a situation you didn't think you'd survive. The point is, you will always surprise yourself, and you will always make it through. Your time is now. You've learned the lessons. You've spent many days and nights waiting for this moment. Now is the time to fully receive what your heart has been asking for. Your patience and dedication are about to pay off big. Your prayers, affirmations, actions, and visualizations are about to materialize into the physical. Everything is about to manifest for you. Be on the lookout. Something major is about to happen for you.

Don't block what's coming by thinking negatively or doubting that it will even happen for you. Doubt, worry, and lack of trust have been slowing down the process. Let go and allow. Start releasing, and start receiving. Greater things are in the works for you. It might seem so difficult and hard when you're dealing with all the challenges and adversities of life, but your faith that the universe will straighten things out will help you remain strong. You may not see it today or tomorrow, but you will look back in a few years and be absolutely perplexed by how every little thing added up and brought you somewhere wonderful, where you always wanted to be. You will be grateful that things didn't work out the way you once wanted them to. In the meantime, just breathe and trust the process.

11. Something great is about to happen for you. Many blessings and new opportunities are about to enter your life. Things are about to start making sense. It's your time. Keep believing. Keep going.

Repeat daily:

I will experience a miracle today.
I am going to get an unexpected positive surprise.
I am blessed.
I am a believer.

Great things are coming for you. So many blessings are headed your way. Your patience, dedication, and trust will be paying off soon. Please know this. Feel it deeply in your heart. Change starts with energy, outlook, belief, and your ability to notice the great things happening around you. Speak it into existence. Believe in it. Always be optimistic, hopeful, and positive that things are going to work out for you.

You Run the Show

Did you know that nothing outside of you really changes—only how you see it? Every single day, your setting looks the same, but on different days, you might be mad, hurt, sad, happy, excited, or joyful. How many emotions have taken place where you are right now? If you take a closer look, it's what you think on the inside that made the reality appear either beautiful or ugly. What you hold internally decides how you see things externally. The only thing changing is you. Now that you have this wisdom, you can start shifting your mindset and changing your attitude to allow blessings to enter your life. Just believe, and let what goes go and what comes come.

Stop Playing the Victim

Don't become a victim of external circumstances, or let what's on the outside control too much of your internal reality. Don't be a puppet to people, situations, or little things that have no real meaning. Don't let your emotions be moved from left to right. Real power lies in self-control. Don't allow your internal state to be easily shifted by external reality. Stand still, hold firm, and decide today that you'll no longer be a button that can easily be pushed for a reaction.

Start Being Grateful

Start counting your blessings now! Being grateful puts the power back in your hands, because you're declaring that you are happy with what you have. This actually frees up a lot of the energy that usually goes into resisting or being angry and unhappy. With gratitude, you can say, "Yes! I love my life!" It's truly a freeing experience. How many things do you love about your life? It doesn't matter how big or small they are—you just need to start saying *thank you*.

12. Sometimes, you just need to relax and remind yourself that you're doing all you can, and everything is going to turn out just fine.

Repeat daily:

I am going to be patient with myself.
I am going to trust the universe even more today.
Everything will work out for me.
I trust myself.

May this message bring you hope, clarity, and positive energy to get you through. Life works in the most beautiful way. Sometimes, we go through ugly moments, but the end story is always a celebration. There will be times in your life when you will feel challenged, with your back against the wall and ready to give up—but it's in these moments that your soul comes alive. The darkest hour brings messages ready to lead you into the light. Be patient with yourself, because there will be times when your soul seems nothing but tired, and your mind tries to pull you back into the darkness from which you have fought so diligently to be free. It is normal, and it is okay. Being genuinely happy and at peace does not mean being in a consistent state of elation.

Don't beat yourself up because you don't wake up with a radiant smile every single day. Understand that being vulnerable to negative emotions is part of being human, and it in no way makes you weak or pathetic. Continue to be patient and kind with yourself. Continue to fight through those draining moments, and do not allow them to persist longer than they should. You are in complete control; sadness is simply a visitor within your mental space, not a permanent resident. Chat with it, understand it, master it—and, most importantly, know when to say goodbye.

Don't give up on yourself. Follow that inner wisdom. Your heart knows, and your spirit has the answers. Tune in! You might not see it now, but everything will fall into place. Whatever is meant to be will happen. It always does. So let go of the excess baggage slowing your transformation, and open yourself to the blessings that are ready to enter your life. You will wake up the next morning, and everything will make sense. Life will make sense. It will all be wonderful. Believe that.

13. Nobody can trigger your emotions without your permission. Learn to be calm and centered no matter what's happening outside of yourself.

Repeat daily:

I choose to be at peace today.
I choose to let go of any emotion that doesn't serve me.
Nothing and nobody can decide how I feel.
I am at ease.

You have to learn how not to be controlled by other people's negativity. You can't walk around with a button that can easily be pushed. You can't be swayed every second by what others outside of you are saying and doing. You have to learn how to be in control of your inner emotions and gain inner stability. Be too great for negativity and nonsense.

Your Emotions

You might not realize this, but you choose how you want to feel. You choose to be sad, happy, excited, up, or down. When people don't understand this, they become reactors. Reactors tie their inner emotions to things, people, situations, and/or circumstances. They wait until *this* happens to be happy. They can't be excited unless *that* happens. Have you noticed that when you're just happy for no reason, people ask, "What are you so happy about?" It's like we can't just be in that state without a reason. And for most people, if there is no reason to be happy, they are either sad or depressed, waiting for something on the outside to shift their inner state.

Start Choosing Your Inner State

The first step is deciding how you want to feel. If you don't decide, you'll be waiting for something on the outside to decide for you. When you make a clear-cut decision, nothing can alter that state as long as you keep your vision on the choice you made. You can have the greatest effect on your reality when you feel good. Feeling good aligns you with the things you desire. The environment might look the same, but the mind looking at it has changed. Know that your inner reality controls your outer reality.

Be Free

I know you might not have been taught this, but you're meant to feel good for no reason. You're meant to be happy for no reason. You're meant to smile for no reason. Let yourself go and be free. You no longer have to wait for these feelings, and you longer have to expect others to give you these feelings. We have to stop tying ourselves down when we're meant to fly.

14. You're in a transformative state. Make room for new energy.

Repeat daily:

I am ready for a big change to happen in my life.
I am aligned for greatness.
I welcome new energy into my life.
I am excited to attract new experiences.

We're all going through a transformative stage. What really matters is keeping up with the change rather than staying stagnant in the old energy. Everything you want out of life starts with you first. Who you are, what you believe in, and how strong your faith is determine the experiences you will have. You're on a mission to be the best version of yourself, and this journey doesn't need any negative baggage. Your dreams don't need doubters. You're planning to fly high, and this time, you're only going to focus on positivity, love, and kindness. You're done with drama, negativity, and overthinking. You're starting to feel deeply committed to your evolution. Your mind and heart are gravitating toward people, things, and situations that help your spiritual development. You're starting to see your truth. You know what you need to do, and you're starting to take action. You're starting to break free from the habits that once drained you. You want to fully live your life. You want to immerse yourself in getting to know who you are. It's all about the self-work. This year, you're totally committed to your development. You know you're going places. You know deep in your heart that you're destined for greatness. You got this. Keep going.

15. Be in a vibrational state that matches what you want to attract. Energy has to align to manifest.

Repeat daily:

I own the state of what I want to manifest.
I am vibrating at a high frequency.
I attract wealth, happiness, and great blessings.
I am blessed, and more blessings find me.

What kind of energy are you putting out into the universe? Are your actions, thoughts, and beliefs aligned with what you want to manifest? Do you own who you want to become? Understand that everything around you is energy. There's a powerful magnetic vibration beaming from your body and mind that is pulling toward you the people, things, and situations currently present in your life. This magnetic pull is your energy signature, matching you to the vibration you hold. If you don't like what you've attracted up to this point, don't stress yourself about it. You can always recreate yourself. Never blame the circumstances; these are just the results of your current thoughts, emotions, and beliefs. You should never blame things on the outside, which will only weaken your personal power to take responsibility for your life.

Instead, focus back on the thoughts, beliefs, and ideas you have about the world. What is that little voice in your head constantly saying? What emotion are you always holding? Your state of being is constantly gravitating everything toward you. Everyone desires change, but to become better, you have to start doing the self-work to overcome any limitations and fears you may hold. You have to start by forgiving yourself and everything outside of yourself first. Forgiveness is a high vibration. It frees you. Did you know that forgiveness means detaching your current precious energy from the past? When you're no longer playing the victim, you allow yourself to transcend into a new space. This space allows you to heal and recreate your vibration to attract new experiences.

At every moment, you have a choice to use your energy to grow your vision, so don't give it away to others or the past to let them benefit from it while you deplete in sorrow. Let go of all the resentments and feel your inner freedom. We're conserving energy here, not tossing it around aimlessly. Once you become detached and own your power, you have the opportunity increase your vibration. The better you become, the better you attract. Everything starts with you!

16. One day, you're just going to be like, "I'm glad I didn't give up back then."

Repeat daily:

I am excited for what the future holds.
I will never give up on my visions.
Every day, I work toward my dreams.
I am happy with where I am, and where I am headed.

One day, you'll look back and be THANKFUL you kept pushing forward. You'll be thankful you kept growing. Reaching that place is making the choice today to keep going, no matter what kind of adversity or challenges you face. Don't let your current situation make you feel hopeless. Remember that one time when you were at a low point, and you made it through? Well, you can do it again! Don't get caught up in this moment and forget your strength. The reason we have all these experiences is not only to get the lessons, but also to become stronger. We're made to survive, adapt, change, and transform ourselves.

Don't hold onto things longer than their stay. Be open to newness, even if it doesn't make sense at the moment. Most of our pain comes from fear of change, because we want what's familiar. We have difficulties letting go because we want to force everything to be the same. The beautiful thing about life is that the moment we let go of what weighs heavily on us, we find new inspiration to continue on. We get a second chance. The best way to get out of a negative cycle is to start working on your thoughts before you work on the outside.

Listen to the predominant thoughts you have—that will give you insight into what you've been attracting. Shift your thoughts to the outcome you want. Change is simple, but it seems complicated when we put most of our focus on what we don't want. Just know that you can, and you will be okay. You've survived before, and you'll survive again. Don't give up on yourself.

17. If you don't renew your mindset and get clear about your vision, you'll just keep recreating the same reality from old thoughts and habits.

Repeat daily:

I am receiving more positive thoughts.
I am getting creative ideas to manifest abundance.
Every day, I am renewed.
I am happy for myself and how much I have grown.

Every day, you make the choice with your thoughts, habits, and behaviors about the direction you want your life to go. Don't get stuck on a few repetitive thoughts and habits that aren't helping you get better. You have a choice to change. You can change your mindset, transform your life, and create new habits. You can decide every single moment how you want to live, and what's in the thoughts you're playing in your mind. You don't need to control them, but you need to pay attention to the common stream of thoughts you're having. Is it negative or positive? Does it make you happy? Or does it put you in a negative cycle that triggers negative emotions? What about your habits—do they support your visions? Are your habits helping you reach your goals?

Once you become aware of your predominant thoughts, you can replace them with thoughts of things you want. Once you decide you don't want to be stuck anymore, you will start to have better habits that align you with your greatest vision. Your thoughts are a force, a frequency, and live energy that you can direct to work for you. You can transform yourself in all areas of your life by focusing and exposing your mind to a lifestyle that matches where you want to be.

What you pay attention to gets magnetized and attracted back to you. You can't have a positive mind and live a negative life. That just goes against the laws of nature. Know this for a fact: the thoughts you entertain, the thoughts you believe in, and the thoughts you hold most of the time are shaping and molding your reality. It's as simple as paying attention to your inner world—your thoughts and emotions. These are the forces that make up your whole reality. Everything in your life right now was once a thought in your mind. Start wearing thoughts that bring you happiness, thoughts that heal, thoughts of prosperity, thoughts of love, and you'll see how much you transform your reality!

18. The reward for all your hard work, all your efforts, all your prayers, and all your visualizations is about to pay off in a major way.

Repeat daily:

The universe rewards me daily.
My thoughts are manifesting quickly.
Everything I do has a high return.
I keep growing and getting better.

It's time for you to RECEIVE. Something you've been praying for is about to happen for you. You've had enough lessons. You've been patient long enough. You've remained strong through many trials and challenges. Nothing has broken you. You're still here, standing strong. Now it's your turn to start receiving blessings, and it is about to happen for you. Things are getting clearer. The answers you need are arriving. The universe is getting ready to make a delivery in your life. In the meantime, celebrate and smile like you've already received everything you have been asking for. I promise it's about to happen for you.

19. Things can get uncomfortable when you're changing and getting better. You're letting go of old habits, limiting beliefs, and fears. Be patient with yourself. No matter what you go through or how hard things get, always believe that better days are coming for you.

Repeat daily:

I allow myself to flow.
I am open to surrender to the universe.
I let go easily and effortlessly.
I believe great things are getting ready to happen for me.

You can't ask for change and expect everything to be the same. You will be moved out of your comfort zone. The process will seem hard. You will feel all types of emotions, and have days when you might feel drained. You might even want to give up and go back to the comfort where you weren't truly happy, but felt "safe."

You can't return, though. You have to welcome the uncomfortable state, because you know your habits are being broken. You know that everything is changing for the better, but at first, you have to shed that old energy. You're in the process of learning a new way of thinking, feeling, and doing this. How can you expect a process like that not to be uncomfortable? The point isn't to stress about how you're feeling, but to be patient with yourself. Guide yourself with kind words. Take your time. Take it one day at a time. Breathe deeply as often as possible. The more you take it one day at a time, the more you'll look back and thank yourself for even moving forward. This is just a reminder that if you're in that space right now, *don't give up*. Be easy on yourself. I'm here with you through this journey to shine a light of hope and positivity on you as you take your steps forward.

20. May all the negative energy that's trying to work against you fail. May you be covered with a protection of light that brings you harmony.

Repeat daily:

I am protected and guided.
I am covered in blessings.
Nothing can stop my positive force.
I am full of love.

Nothing and nobody can stop your blessings. They can try all they want, but they don't have control over your reality. You do. Knowing this will empower your life, because you'll no longer think in a lack mindset or be a victim of external reality. You won't allow anyone to make you think that you do not deserve what you're about to manifest. You will believe in yourself, and know that nothing and nobody can get in the way of what you visualize or dream of. You have full power to dictate the reality you want to experience. All that's needed is for you to start believing in yourself and never give up on your vision. Start living in your light, and keep glowing in positivity as you effortlessly manifest your reality.

21. There is a future version of you who has manifested everything you have always dreamed of, and is proud that you were strong enough to make it.

Repeat daily:

I have manifested everything I have always desired.
Today, I will celebrate my manifestations.
I manifest daily.
I attract so many blessings into my life.

Look at it this way: everything you're currently doing is the past that you'll be talking about in your future. At the same time, everything you're currently doing is the future you'll be living. How you choose to live in this moment is what creates your past and your future. The funny thing is, a lot of us are stuck in the past or the future, not realizing that *now* is the only time we truly have to create our lives.

How to free your mind from the past:

A lot of people haven't learned the art of letting go, the art of forgiveness, and the art of acceptance. Many people carry around too many regrets, hold onto grudges, and carry around loads of mistakes. Understand one thing clearly: you can't change what has already happened. You have to learn to stop victimizing yourself and let go. You have to free your mind from the weight of the past. Good or bad, your past experiences occurred to mature you, not to keep you stuck. Forgive yourself for them, accept what happened, and gracefully let go. You have better things to be creating with your mind right now.

How to free your mind from the future:

The future isn't some distant place, like it seems in your mind. The future is right now. It's actually funny that so many people are sitting around thinking that someday, out of nowhere, the future will happen to them. This is why so many feel like they haven't accomplished many of their goals—because they are living in the future in their minds, rather than right now. What you do right now will be your future. How you take care of your mind and body today will be your future. The amount of energy you put into bettering yourself now will be your future.

Your present life is a gift:

If you want to attract something, you have to be in that state right now. If you want to be successful, you must have a successful mindset now. If your mind is not in the present, you're missing out on changing your life. Start refocusing on what you're doing moment to moment, and see how much power you have to alter your reality completely.

22. Don't go back to your old ways. Toxic habits, people, and energy always try to come back when you're doing better. Stay focused.

Repeat daily:

I refuse to look back.
I have so many great things happening for me.
I am attracting great people into my life.
I am happy with where I am, and how much I have grown.

When you're growing and getting better, things return to test you. These can be old habits, people, and situations you're no longer a part of. This is the process of growth, because when you take care of yourself and prioritize your happiness, you start to glow and shine. The energy you emit becomes magnetic and makes you more attractive. You have to keep your vibration high, and keep going. Keep getting better. Keep entering higher levels of growth. It's not about showing off, or proving a point to anyone. It's about your own inner wellness. Stay focused on that.

23. When you start taking care of yourself, you start feeling better. You start looking better, and you even start to attract better. Everything starts with you.

Repeat daily:

I feel good about my new way of thinking.
Things just keep getting better and better for me.
Every day, I do something to improve myself.
I keep evolving and growing.

Be so busy becoming the best version of yourself that you don't have time or energy to involve yourself in negativity, drama, the past, or things that drain you. Be defined by what you do, not what others have done to you. Don't give people that kind of power over you.

The better you become, the better you attract:

Every moment, you have the choice to use your energy to grow your vision, so don't give it away to others or the past to benefit from, while you deplete in sorrow. Let go of all the could haves, should haves, and *he or she did this to me* nonsense. Stop letting others weigh you down. Stop overthinking everything. We're conserving energy here, not tossing it around aimlessly. Once you become detached and own your power, you'll have the opportunity increase your vibration.

Be busy succeeding:

Start taking care of your mind by having more positive, optimistic thoughts. Take care of your body so you can feel good. Take care of your soul by filling it with love and laughter. Succeed in every area of your life. When you do the self-work and bring the energy back to yourself, you'll notice your life will start to transform for the better. You'll no longer be worried, because you have an inner trust that everything is working out for the best. Everything that once held you down will now be a stepping stone to reaching your highest goals.

Elevate yourself:

You have to learn to elevate yourself so you don't lower your vibration and stay stagnant. You have to know what you deserve, not just by thought alone, but by action, too. When you set the bar for how you want to be treated, people will follow.

Let go:

Never identify yourself by something that happened in the past. If you're the conscious creator of your life, you know that each moment transpires according to how you view yourself. Instead of linking your potential to the past, how about letting go of it, and living how you want to be today? Don't give people from your past power over who you can be today. Nothing can limit you except for what you allow. Decide to be happy. Decide to get better. Decide to mature and gain wisdom.

24. Don't worry if you don't see the changes right away. Your mental reality is shifting, and soon, your outer reality will match.

Repeat daily:

My mind is changing, and my reality is getting better.
I am saying my positive thoughts out loud to manifest my reality.
When I believe in something, it happens for me.
I trust the universe to provide for me.

We're so stressed out these days, because we believe everything needs to happen right now. We forget that everything happens in perfect timing. We always want everything to happen instantly. If we don't see anything changing on the outside, we start to lose faith in the power to manifest our reality. We might even start doubting if it's real, or possible.

You can't plant the seed and instantly pull it out to see if anything is growing. Your role now is to water the thoughts, habits, and beliefs you want to manifest externally. Soon, you will see what you've planted come to fruition. We have to be more patient and trusting as we are doing our inner work. You are making a lot of changes in your life, and the energy of your mind, body, and soul is shifting to a higher frequency to align you with new experiences, new habits, new people, new energy, and a whole new mindset.

Everything will suddenly change for you. It will all happen. However, your number one focus right now is to continue making the changes and not give up on yourself. Keep watering your seed. Give yourself the space you need to reconnect with your inner self. Keep reminding yourself why you even wanted to change in the first place.

Deep down within your soul, you knew you deserved more out of life than what you used to settle for. Now that you're going to be more patient, you'll be allowing the work to be done through you and for you. Soon, you will notice the results of your efforts. You will see how powerful you are. You will notice that you have the ability to fully transform your life. Give yourself credit right now. You're on a beautiful journey.

25. Don't share your visions until they manifest. This keeps doubters and people with negative energy from knowing too much.

Repeat daily:

I trust that my visions will manifest.
I am too great to doubt myself.
I focus my mental energy to get what I want.
My thoughts manifest really quickly.

Don't tell people your plans—show them your results. Many people struggle with this concept, because they easily share their visions and expect others to understand them. They get discouraged if someone doesn't believe in them. They start doubting themselves, and even start to become fearful. People who don't believe in themselves kill so many visions and dreams. It starts off with someone having an idea that is unthinkable to the next person. The reason you received that vision is because you're able to tap into that level of possibility. You literally tune into what you believe is possible for you. It's different for everyone. This can mean that the next person might not be able to fully believe in themselves until they start to realize that they are a soul that is boundless and limitless. When someone tells you that something is not possible, they are just saying it's not possible for them right now.

When someone is unconscious of their true potential, they project life from a limited point of view. That's not how things work when you're operating on the realm of consciously creating your reality. In this sacred place, everything is abundant, and there's no limit to what you can do, achieve, or have. Since most people haven't tapped into this level of belief, they easily share their lack and try to taint open minds from seeing clearly. This is where you have to become strong and realize the power in keeping silent. We don't see the work of the seed under the dirt until the plant flourishes. In silence, you pull the creative force to your work rather than scattering it and opening it up for judgment. Once your vision beautifully buds, everyone will notice. Without a single word, you not only materialize your vision, but you also give hope to those who have a hard time believing in themselves.

26. My mind is the universe. Everything I visualize will come to life. Everything I believe in will manifest for me.

Repeat daily:

I am connected to the universe.
I believe in the power of the universe to assist me in manifesting my dreams.
I can make anything I want happen.
The possibilities are endless for me.

I believe in the power of my mind. Everything I imagine has the potential to be my reality. The clearer my visions are, the faster I experience them. Connecting my emotions with my visions is a catalyst to receiving what my heart desires. I have to feel it. I have to believe it before I see it. I know everything around me stemmed from a single thought. I trust the process, because I know the Law of Gestation states that everything planted is in a state of fruition.

I'm starting to spend more time understanding how my mind works. There's truly a vast power within all of us, and the only way we can tap into it is to go on an inner journey. You are not your mistakes, your past, your shortcomings, or anything that makes you feel low. The point is to vibrate higher and increase your energy so you can feel at peace. The pain and confusion come from forgetting what we truly are. We're magical beings with vast power. Our thoughts, imagination, and how we create through our visions are enough to let you know and believe that you're much more than you think.

Nobody teaches you these things, because the standards of physical reality are solely objective. The pressure to fit into ideals, to be accepted, or to be approved of lowers your self-worth and makes you further disconnect from your soul. The more time you spend unlearning or disconnecting from negativity, doubts, and fears, the more powerful you become. You have to be committed to understanding yourself and learning to heal, open, and access your heart.

The burdens we carry are an illusion. We keep them real because we continue to repeat them in our minds. We continue to tell that same story to others and to ourselves. The more we think it, the more we feel it, and the more we experience it in our external reality. It's time to just let go. Recreate yourself. I learned to accept that I'm different, and I'm going to own it unapologetically. This starts the freeing process. Spend every day transforming yourself. Commit to a better you. Meditate, visualize, and see how powerful you are. Trust that what you hold in your mind will come to reality.

27. For once, stop and thank yourself for how far you've come. You've been trying to make changes in your life, and all your effort counts.

Repeat daily:

I am doing the best I can.
I work on myself daily.
I congratulate myself for all my accomplishments.
I give myself credit.

We really don't give ourselves enough credit. We work so hard to get to where we are, only to feel like we're not there yet. This is a vicious cycle that can make you chase the next moment instead of embracing how far you've come. Take credit for trying. Take credit for your progress. The little things matter. We always think that success means the final result, or a sudden leap from where you are to where you want to be. The baby steps, the small accomplishments, and the days when you want to give up can be difficult, but the fact that you try a little harder is what counts. This is a sign for you, a sign to not give up on yourself and a sign of hope. Give yourself credit. You are trying, and you are a work in progress. I just wanted to say that I am proud of you. Keep going!

28. You become a master of your life when you learn how to control where your attention goes. Value what you give your energy to.

Repeat daily:

I focus my energy on what matters.
I value my time.
I give my attention to what adds value to my life.
I am happy with what I am attracting.

You're donating the time of your existence to the things you give your attention to. Make sure that what's taking your energy is worth your life. There are just too many distractions going on. I consider anything that doesn't grow you, evolve you, and make you better a distraction. How many more years will go by just doing the same old thing? We all have the same 24 hours, but what makes us so different is how we choose to invest our time. The biggest asset you have is your attention. Anyone who is aware understands that attention is energy. How you use this powerful energy will determine the kind of reality you experience.

Start focusing your mental energy by doing things that you need to get done first. Don't put off the joy of creating the vision you want by doing things that aren't adding any real long-term value to your life.

Anytime you're doing something, ask yourself: *How is this benefiting my life?* This is the fastest way to realize if you're being distracted or wasting time. Start investing in your life: read more often, relax to connect with your inner self, question everything, be aware, be curious, explore reality, create your ideas, and expand yourself so you can learn something new. Become the change you want to manifest in your life.

29. I surrender and let go of what doesn't belong in my life to make room for the arrival of great blessings. It's all about being patient and trusting the divine timing of things. The universe will bless me, because I radiate energy that's aligned with what I'm asking for.

Repeat daily:

I love everything that is happening in my life.
Things get easier for me daily.
I am flowing and allowing.
I let the universe guide me.

"What you resist persists!" Most pain comes from resisting the universal flow to actually bless your life with the unimaginable. Surrender and let go. Just release all the negative energy, the negative thoughts from the past, the hurt, the pain, and the confusion. When you decide to surrender and let go, you're sending a message that you're ready for change to happen in your life. This is a powerful moment and a magical time. Everything you want out of life starts happening.

Resisting

Suffering comes from resisting the change to move forward and flow. The ego makes you believe that you are separate from everything, and automatically puts you in a state that resists change. The ego is purely physical in terms of thought patterns, and pretty much stays on the surface. Its concerns are usually petty problems dramatized in the mind. Forgetting your true nature in this manner disconnects you from yourself, and makes you a slave to circumstances. When you don't trust in your higher power's process to put you at ease, you resist flowing with life. Being in this kind of state causes you so much pain because you feel hopeless. Don't be fooled by your ego. You are much more powerful than you think. You are connected; you always were, and always will be. Only your thoughts make you believe you aren't.

Life's Flow

Have you noticed when you just surrender or let go of something, things just start to fall into place? Well, that's the power of life's flow. The moment you let go, you restore your ability to see clearly. You become creative, and able to discover solutions you could never have seen before. Most of us get to this state when we're just tired of going against the flow, so we surrender from exhaustion. However, this flow is forever present. You can connect with it by shifting your mind from attachments, resistance, and overthinking to letting go, accepting, and trusting in the process. Choose inner peace. Choose to flow.

30. I will eliminate all negative thoughts that try to enter my mind.

Repeat daily:

Positivity flows through my mind.
I am filled with positive thoughts.
My mind guides me to notice the blessings around me.
I attract good energy.

There's nothing worse than overthinking and drowning in your own thoughts. Negative thinking can deplete you and take over your emotions, keeping you stuck in a cycle you don't want to be in. The good news is that the thoughts occurring in your mind can be changed once you realize that you're in charge of what goes on in your head.

Why you might be stuck:

First things first: understand that you have a choice in what you think. Yes—you decide every moment what plays in your mind. This step will help you take responsibility and provide insights for getting out of the rut and taking back the control you need to be internally stable. When people don't realize that they have this kind of power to choose what they think, they start to become the thoughts rather than deciding the thoughts. If you don't decide your own thoughts, your environment, the people in your life, and your circumstances and situations will rent space in your head and decide for you. This is where a lot of people feel consumed and drained by their thoughts, because they don't realize that they run the show. Your internal reality belongs to you. It's not a button for external reality to push at any given moment. Take back control.

Patterns and Progression

There's a pattern in how this cycle of overthinking or entertaining negative, draining thoughts occurs. Let's say you see something you don't like. Quickly, your outer environment triggers internal thoughts to take place. The thoughts trigger an emotion, and the emotion re-triggers the thoughts. Even though the outer experience is over, it still lives on internally, because people live in their thoughts. They may dissect the scenario a million and one ways, only to drain themselves. This is why someone can be stuck on something that happened to him or her years ago—because they haven't realized they can break the thought cycle. To avoid becoming consumed by your thoughts, always ask yourself: *Is this thought beneficial to my inner wellness?* Once you start to choose what you're thinking and deciding what stays in your mind, that's when you become free and realize that you are not your thoughts.

31. I have to study myself. I want to get to know who I am and identify my purpose.

Repeat daily:

I am investing more energy into getting better.
I learn something new every day.
I am patient and loving with myself.
I expand my mind and connect with myself daily.
The only thing I'm committed to right now
is bettering myself.

Work on yourself, focus on you, and you will see how much your life changes. I've gained so much inner peace learning that I need to prioritize myself first. No decision will pay off more than giving extreme focus and energy to the things with the highest return. When you're doing self-work, you have to eliminate things that are keeping you blind from your truth. You can't be afraid of rebirth. You have to let go and be hungry for change.

Distractions

There are just too many distractions going on. I consider anything that doesn't grow you, evolve you, and make you better a distraction. How many more years will go by with you doing the same old thing? We all have the same 24 hours, but what makes us so different is how we choose to invest our time. The biggest asset you have is your attention. Anybody who is aware of the self understands that attention is energy. It's more powerful than currency. It controls it! How you use this powerful energy will determine the kind of reality you experience.

Realize this:

Your attention is being diverted from you when you invest your time and attention in aimless conversations, purposeless events, and negative people who have no goals. Many people are doing meaningless things to fill the void of inner emptiness. You can't avoid who you are. You have to get to know yourself. Understand your life. Find your purpose and be motivated to make changes today, so you can be thankful for years to come.

Invest in your life:

Anytime you're doing something, ask yourself: How is this benefiting my life? This is the fastest way to realize if you're being distracted or wasting time. Start investing in your life. Read more often, relax to connect with your inner self, question everything, be aware, be curious, explore reality, create your ideas, and gain knowledge to apply. Your time is now!

32. When you start seeing your worth, you'll find it hard to stay around people who don't.

Repeat daily:

I am worthy of receiving what my heart desires.
I value myself and respect my time.
I focus my energy on what I want.
I don't tolerate any negativity in my life.

The more we become aware of who we are, the more we start to realize our worth and take back our personal power. We awaken from the negative mindset of unworthiness, and transform from the need to be accepted. Once you realize what you're made of, nobody can ever define it for you.

Why We Feel Unworthy

Some people feel unworthy because they have allowed society to dictate who they are. We're constantly told to seek approval, to be in competition, and to chase happiness. In the mist of doing all of this, we lose ourselves. We start to attract others who also don't know their self-worth, and we try to do anything to be accepted by them, even if we're unhappy. This mental conditioning seems normal in our society, but internally, we feel empty. Our light starts to dim. We've become so objective in everything we do, we forget what we're made of. Nobody teaches you to approve of yourself, to love yourself, to get to know yourself, and to connect back to where it all stems from: you!

Finding Your Worth

You're not defined by anything on the outside. Don't waste your time trying to be accepted by others, or trying to live up to standards that are making you lose yourself even more. The most important person that matters is you. You are the one who determines your true self-worth. Instead of focusing so much on outer reality, give some attention to where the creation of reality takes place: your inner self. The quality of your thoughts is everything.

Eliminate and replace negative thoughts with positive ones. Start loving yourself completely. Stop comparing your life, your growth, your process, and your journey to others. So much of the energy you could be using to create your reality is wasted in judging, comparing, and condemning yourself. It's time to switch it up.

Realization

Once you have awakened to your truth, you'll be empowered to make choices that uplift, inspire, and change you for the better. You'll start to feel lighter, freer, and happier with yourself. You'll start to attract others who also know their worth, and suddenly, life becomes a pleasure rather than a burden.

33. More blessings come in when I decide to focus on what's right in my life instead of what's wrong.

Repeat daily:

I am blessed.
I am blessed.
I am blessed.
I am blessed.

My favorite thing to do when I wake up or before I go to bed is to count my blessings. I don't care what kinds of challenges I'm facing. My reality isn't what's happening, but rather what I'm focusing on. I know my power is in my energy. Instead of seeing problems, I decide to focus on every little thing in my life that's blooming. Remember that attention is energy. Thoughts are energy. Words are energy. Emotions are energy. How you use the combination determines what you experience in your reality. You decide what you want to notice. Now is the time for you to switch it up. Don't give away your power to lack, low vibrations, negativity, or drama any longer. Renew your focus. You can "rewire" your brain to be happy simply by recalling three things you're grateful for every day for 21 days.

34. I am attracting my own vibrations. If I see something I don't like, I check myself and make sure that it's not what I'm reflecting.

Repeat daily:

Everything starts with me.
I am responsible for what I attract.
I focus on getting better.
I am patient with myself.

A definite sign of maturity and growth is when you start to take responsibility for the reality you're creating, the mistakes you've made, and the energy you hold. If something in your life is causing you a lot of problems or unrest, try not to look outward, and try not to blame circumstances. Instead, direct your energy to figuring out which kinds of thoughts and emotions you're currently entertaining. Everything starts with your thoughts. Our minds are on a constant search to align us with exactly what we're looking for. If you seem to find yourself in constant health-related, financial, and/or relationship discordance, it's probably due to the fact that you're tuning into a frequency that doesn't align with what you really want. Wanting something is just not enough to experience it. Most people say they want one thing, but tune their emotions, energy, and thoughts to the negative aspect of what they desire out of life. This is where training your mind comes into play.

Here are several reasons why you might not be experiencing your dream as your reality:

1. **Habits.** This is a big one, because this is your comfort zone. This is where most people fail at getting what they want. You can't be in the old habits and desire new outcomes. You have to break the cycle. Try something new. Be open!
2. **Pessimistic attitude.** Train your mind to be optimistic and ambitious. Have faith. Start finding the good in things.
3. **Negative self-talk.** This is a dream killer and an energy-depleting habit. If you haven't trained your thoughts, the same old record of *I can't, I'm not good enough*, or *it won't work for me* is continuously play-

ing in your mind. End this negative self-talk by saying something positive about yourself each time that voice surfaces. In due time, you'll rewire your train of thought. With minor changes come major results. Alignment to what you want is only a few lifestyle adjustments away. Start living your dream; the possibilities are endless!

35. Something within you is starting to detect that there's a deeper meaning to life.

Repeat daily:

The universe continuously provides me with signs.
I am a spirit and a powerful being.
My energy is valuable.
My life is worthy.

If you're currently becoming more conscious of your environment, don't be afraid to embrace your realization. You might notice a lot of patterns, beliefs, activities, and behaviors you no longer agree with dissolving. You might start to realize that you are much more than the mundane cycles of everyday living. You might be at a point where you want to know your real purpose. You might even feel uncomfortable during this time of transition. You're not alone, but it might feel like you are.

When we're becoming more conscious of our lives, we start to see things differently. It might feel weird for some people, and liberating for others. The transition to accepting your true self will require you to shed your past fears, beliefs, and thought patterns that were keeping you stuck. The whole point is to realize your power and your worth, and to realize that everything starts and ends with you. So many years of objectifying our lives made us want to be accepted, loved, and approved of by others. However, when you go inside and awaken to your truth, you'll become the things you love, admire, and require in your life. Rather than looking out, you'll suddenly start to attract it by being it.

The paradox of life is that you get everything when you become it, not when you chase it and try so hard. There's beauty in stillness, allowing, and letting go. This is something we're all learning and working on. Don't slow down your growth by trying to hold onto people, things, and habits that are no longer serving you. Start becoming okay with your changes. Start to accept that everyone is evolving on his or her own terms. This is the time for you to do your self-work. Tune in and create the peace, love, and joy you search for. Life happens the moment we allow and just flow. Start shining your inner light.

14

AFFIRM IT

100 Affirmations That Will Help You Start Speaking, Feeling, and Commanding Greatness, Abundance, Happiness, and Financial Freedom in Your Life

"It's the repetition of affirmations that leads to belief. And once that belief becomes a deep conviction, things begin to happen." — *Muhammad Ali*

Affirmations are one of the most powerful tools you can use during your manifestation process. The words you constantly repeat to yourself, silently or out loud, have great power to influence the reality you create. Words have a powerful frequency behind them; they carry an energy that can alter your reality completely. The reality you create daily depends upon the words you use to express yourself. Are you using words that can help you or harm you? Are your words empowering, motivating, or uplifting? Do you have positive self-talk, or negative self-talk? Once you become aware of this power, you'll start to use it to help change your life and completely alter your reality in a positive way.

The more we understand the power of our words, the more we can take practical steps to use them for our benefit rather than destroying ourselves or limiting our creations. The power of sound conditions your mind to constantly experience what you speak. The words you speak to others or yourself can actually be weakening your vibration and causing you not to feel good about yourself.

You will start to create the habit of consciously becoming aware of how you speak to yourself by using these affirmations to empower yourself every single day. Your words guide your mind and body toward the experiences you want to have. Use your words to empower yourself. Become aware of what you're constantly telling yourself. Affirm exactly what you want to experience. Say it out loud to yourself. Change the words you speak, and everything around you will change.

I have put together 100 affirmations that will supercharge your energy so you can reprogram your mind and shift your reality. These affirmations will help guide you and keep your energy on track as you raise your frequency to become the ultimate magnetic manifestor. When you start to speak these new words, you'll notice that how you feel will begin to change. The goal is to constantly repeat the affirmations and connect each one with an emotion. Feel the power of the words completely taking over your mind and body. This is a great way to charge your energy and feel good about yourself. If, for some reason, the words don't seem believable enough, try to remember that you are reprogramming your mind to positivity and a new way of thinking. Resistance can come from a lack of self-belief, which is why you must keep repeating the words until you own the new energy that's going to empower your life.

It's time for you to consciously start using the frequencies of your words to change what you think, feel, and attract. You have the power to completely alter your reality. Start speaking greatness, abundance, love, and financial freedom into existence.

Own Your Greatness **Affirmations**

"Greatness is not a function of circumstance. Greatness, it turns out, is largely a matter of conscious choice, and discipline." — James C. Collins

This set of affirmations will help you remember that you were born great. Everything about you is perfect right now. No matter what has happened in the past or how you feel about yourself right now, it is time for you to own your greatness by using the power of affirmations. The shift in your words and how you'll start to speak to yourself right now will charge your energy and allow you to feel deserving of everything you want to manifest. In order to receive, you must first own the state. YOU ARE GREAT. No matter what you've been told before by others or even yourself, today is the day that you will shift those negative mental thought patterns to ones of greatness and a frequency of higher power that will remind you of your truth.

1. I AM GREAT.

I am GREAT! My life is GREAT! Everything is happening for me. All the things that I am currently experiencing are only taking me to the next level of my life. I am growing. I am getting better. I choose to believe in sudden miracles and unexpected blessings.

2. I WAS BORN TO DO GREAT THINGS.

I am here for a reason. I have a purpose. I am going to allow the universe to give me a sign because I am ready to receive the guidance to do all that I can. The answers I need are deep within me, and I know they are coming out daily even more clearly. I was born, aligned, and am here to do great things. I believe in myself.

3. I AM TOO GREAT TO SETTLE FOR LESS.

I am way too great to be settling for less. I have to recognize that I am valuable and worthy already. I was born that way. Everything I need is within me right now. The answers are all there. Everything starts with me. I am going to tap into my inner powers and create the reality I want. I am way too powerful to be settling for less.

4. I OWN MY GREATNESS.

I own my greatness without having to explain it. I am just going to be it. I am feeling good about my ideas, creativity, and genius frequency. I have an unlimited connection with universal energy that provides the answers I need. If I am connected, nothing and no one can stop my shine. I am GREAT!

5. GREAT BLESSINGS BELONG IN MY LIFE.

Since I am in the frequency of greatness, I am only attracting great blessings. How I feel attracts what I experience, so from now on, I am only going to feel the powerful energy of greatness surrounding me in all ways.

I Feel Good About Myself/I Love Myself **Affirmations**

"To love oneself is the beginning of a lifelong romance." — Oscar Wilde

The next set of affirmations is so important, because how you feel about yourself and your internal dialogue with regard to who you are is what makes you feel worthy and deserving of receiving the best life has to offer. The frequency of self-love will empower you to know that you are good enough already. This energy is a great way to uplift your spirit when you get into a moment of comparing yourself or doubting your self-worth.

6. I AM GOOD ENOUGH.

I am good enough already. I already have the seed of creation within me that powers my life and makes me whole. My power is in tuning in and recognizing that I am good enough already, and I can do anything I put my mind to.

7. I LOVE MYSELF.

I love who I am. I am not waiting for anyone to validate me or give me permission to be who I was born to be. Everything starts with how I feel about myself, and today, I will choose to love myself even more, because loving myself is the highest frequency that attracts, aligns, and connects everything. I believe in myself. I love myself.

8. I BELIEVE IN MYSELF.

I believe in myself.

I am powerful.

I can do great things.

I can overcome any hardship.

I am unstoppable.

9. I ACCEPT MYSELF.

I accept who I am. I will not judge myself or compare myself to anyone.

10. I RADIATE POSITIVE ENERGY.

I shine from the inside.

I glow with self-love.

I have so much positive energy coming out of me that I feel it all over my body. It feels good to radiate positive energy. It feels good to know that I can access, project, and spread this high frequency from within me, anytime and anywhere.

11. I GLOW WITH LOVE.

I have a powerful magnetic energy of love that attracts the highest frequency of love from all over the universe. I feel a rush of energy and unconditional love that surrounds me and nurtures me. I am full of love. I have so much love to give. I have so much love to share. I am free. I am filled.

12. I LOVE MY LIFE.

I love my life.

I love my body.

I love how much I am growing and getting better.

Everything in my life is working out for my greatest good.

I am aligned, connected, and provided for.

I feel so good about myself.

My life is what I make it. I have the power to change everything. I have the power right now to love myself and accept who I am.

13. I AM GOING TO TAKE CARE OF MYSELF.

I am going to start prioritizing my happiness and eliminating everything from my life that isn't good for me. I have to take care of myself. I have to prioritize my mental, physical, and spiritual wellness. I don't ever have to settle.

14. I AM GOING TO BE FIRM ABOUT WHAT I DESERVE.

I know my value. I know my worth. I know what I deserve. I will never settle. I will never allow myself to dim my light. I am too great, too loving, and too powerful to doubt myself.

15. LOVING MYSELF MULTIPLIES MY MANIFESTATION ABILITIES.

If I feel good, and I attract great things. If I feel happy, I attract great things. Everything starts with my energy state. I know the power of loving myself is what helps me manifest faster. I choose to be filled, covered, and surrounded by love. The highest frequency of the universe nurtures me, supports me, and provides for me. I am LOVED.

I AM Manifesting What I Want **Affirmations**

"My imagination creates my reality." — *Walt Disney*

These next affirmations will keep you on track as you are manifesting what you want. These words are charged with an energy that will make you feel abundant, limitless, and completely unstoppable.

16. I AM A MAGNETIC MANIFESTOR.

I am a magnetic manifestor who easily and effortlessly attracts everything I want. I can pull anything my heart desires to myself through my thoughts. I am a magnet to all my manifestations.

17. I FEEL MY MANIFESTATIONS RUSHING TOWARD ME.

My manifestations are rushing toward me. They are being pulled to me at a high rate of speed. I feel the energy of what I want to manifest on the way. It is arriving. The universe is making a big delivery in my life. I can just feel it. I believe it. It is finally here. That was extremely fast.

18. I AM ATTRACTING GREAT ABUNDANCE.

I am attracting great abundance, prosperity, positive connections, and unlimited wisdom that will guide me in the right direction to create a fulfilling life.

19. I CREATE MY OWN REALITY.

I am a creator of my reality. Everything starts with my imagination, thoughts, and feelings. I will start thinking the thoughts I want to manifest. I will start feeling the feelings I want to manifest. I will imagine, visualize, and see everything already manifesting for me. It's all happening for me right now.

20. I AM LIMITLESS.

I am limitless. I can dream, visualize, and be anything I want to be. There are no blocks or limitations in this vast universe. There are no blocks or limitations in my life. I live in a magical world that is filled with mystery, balance, and precise order. The universe does everything in great balance. I am aligned to this limitless frequency.

21. I SEE MY MANIFESTATIONS.

I see my manifestations before they happen. I see them in my mind first. The details of the images are clear. I feel the energy of my visions coming to life. Once I think it, it is already on the way. My manifestations are coming to me right now. They are arriving.

22. THE "HOW" IS NOT MY BUSINESS.

How things are going to happen is not my business. All I need to focus on is what I want. All I need to think about is what I want. All I need to feel is what I want. The universe will take care of the *how*. The universe will provide me the signs, answers, and guidance I need to take the steps toward my visions. I trust the universe.

23. I JUMP FOR JOY!

I jump, dance, sing, and celebrate with joy, because everything I want has literally happened for me. It has all manifested! I believed in the end vision, and it has happened. I saw the picture clearly, and it has manifested. The power of my mind is so magical.

24. I ONLY SPEAK, THINK, AND FEEL WHAT I WANT TO MANIFEST.

I am using my words, thoughts, and feelings to charge my manifestations. Every time I speak, I will speak the energy that supports my vision and what I want. I will use my thoughts and emotions to charge the words I speak. From now on, I will only speak, think, and feel what I want to manifest.

25. I TRUST THAT THE UNIVERSE WILL PROVIDE FOR ME.

I am not going to worry, stress, or overthink how something will happen for me. I will simply trust the universe to provide for me.

26. I ALREADY CLAIM, OWN, AND BELIEVE THE BLESSINGS THAT ARE COMING MY WAY.

I am living my life as if everything I want to manifest has already happened. I am grateful for what I have manifested. What a wonderful life this is! I am just so thankful for how quickly everything is happening for me.

27. I AM PREPARED TO RECEIVE WHAT I AM ASKING FOR.

I match the energy of what I want by being what I want. I step into this state now, and own it as mine.

28. I AM GOING TO SPEAK EVERYTHING INTO EXISTENCE.

My words are so powerful that from now on, when I speak, I will speak the language of manifesting. I am going to speak into existence financial, mental, spiritual, and physical stability. I will speak, be, and attract love, success, friendship, happiness, inner peace, and clarity. All will manifest for me.

29. I AM NOT GOING TO RUSH ANYTHING.

I know everything I want to manifest will happen through patience and trust. When I send my intentions out, I'm just going to chill out and believe that everything is in the works. I will do my part when the universe gives me the signs and aligns me.

30. MY MIND IS THE UNIVERSE.

My mind is the universe.

Everything I visualize will come to life.

Everything I believe in will manifest for me.

31. EVERYTHING I WANT ALREADY EXISTS IN THE UNIVERSE.

What I want already exists. It's not hard to get it. I just have to align with it by matching the frequency of what I want and surrounding myself with the energy of what I want. I read books, talk to people, and do things that match the frequency of the life I want to live. I am stepping up my vibration.

32. EVERY DAY, I WILL REPEAT TO MYSELF:

What I want to manifest has arrived.

What I want to manifest has arrived.

What I want to manifest has arrived.

What I want to manifest has arrived.

33. MY THOUGHTS MANIFEST INSTANTLY.

The thoughts I want to manifest come into my reality instantly. I see everything I think about all around me.

34. I MANIFEST EASILY AND EFFORTLESSLY.

I get what I want easily and effortlessly. I always believe that things happen for me, and that the universe is working for me. I am just so excited to constantly receive great blessings and unexpected surprises.

35. NOTHING AND NOBODY CAN STOP MY MANIFESTATIONS.

I believe that I will manifest my greatest dreams. Nothing and nobody can get in the way of what's meant for me. There is plenty for everyone to have everything they want. There is no competition. There is no lack. The universe provides for everyone, just like the air we breathe.

36. I EXPECT SUDDEN MIRACLES.

Dear Universe, SURPRISE ME!

I AM Manifesting FINANCIAL FREEDOM to Do ANYTHING I Want

"All of the money that you want is available for you to receive. All you have to do is allow it into your experience." — *Abraham Hicks*

The next set of affirmations will charge your energy to start manifesting more money, creativity, and opportunities into your life. The frequency of money is abundance, and the more you feel that energy, the more you align with the infinite supply that will pour in unlimited amounts into your life.

37. I LOVE RECEIVING MONEY.

I have a good relationship with money. Money buys me the experiences I want. The more I feel good about receiving money, the more it comes into my life.

38. MONEY FLOWS INTO MY LIFE.

No matter what is going on, I always notice that money easily and effortlessly flows into my life. I get more than I need, and the supply never stops.

39. MY INCOME DOUBLES, TRIPLES, AND QUADRUPLES CONSTANTLY.

My income keeps growing. I keep getting opportunities to make lots of money.

40. I SPEND FREELY, BECAUSE I RECEIVE ABUNDANTLY.

I buy what I love without thinking about money. Every time I spend money, it comes back to me very quickly, and in increasing amounts.

41. I AM RICH WITH CREATIVE IDEAS.

I have great ideas that can make me lots of money. I have to start sharing my talents and what I am good at with the world, so I can create a positive flow of abundance. I am so rich in ideas that provide value to many people.

42. THE UNIVERSE PROVIDES FOR ME.

If there is a will, there is a way. The universe rewards me with lots of money by setting me up with the perfect opportunities to do what I love and get paid for it.

43. MY BUSINESS ATTRACTS A LOT OF PEOPLE.

So many people are showing up to pay me for my services, talents, and time. People are being aligned to me right now so I can help them and get paid doing it.

44. MONEY FLOWS IN LARGE AMOUNTS RIGHT INTO MY BANK ACCOUNT.

Money comes to me from all over the place, and it shows up unexpectedly. The flow never stops. The money never stops. I check my balance, and it keeps increasing. I am so happy to be in the money flow.

45. I KEEP FINDING MONEY ON THE GROUND.

Everywhere I walk, I see money. I see money all over the place. I notice it on the ground, and I pick it up and thank the universe for providing for me.

46. I BUY WHAT I WANT, WHEN I WANT.

I imagine the universe giving me the key to all abundance, and I never worry about how I will be provided for. I spend money with the frequency of knowing that so much more is entering my account as I am spending. I am in the flow. I have no worries. I am free.

47. I GIVE MONEY.

I have so much money that I give it away to people. I surprise them with a gift or an unexpected payment. I put the frequency I am getting back out into the universe. I keep the flow going.

48. PEOPLE WANT TO SUPPORT MY IDEAS.

People are coming into my life who want to buy, support, and invest in what I am selling. They show up daily, and they love the value I offer. I am so happy that I am putting good energy into the universe and getting paid for it. Life is so good.

49. THE UNIVERSE PAYS ME FOR MY VISIONS.

I am rewarded, paid, and provided for by the universe. I am put in the right place at the right time to get more money and create more value for humanity. My ideas, visions, and creativity make me so much money. I am going to put more energy into providing value, and let the universe take care of the rest.

50. I AM CONNECTED TO THE INFINITE SUPPLY.

Like the vast sky and the ocean and all the living things within it, I am also connected to the infinite supply that effortlessly provides for all. As long as I am breathing, I am provided for in this reality.

51. I NOTICE ABUNDANCE EVERYWHERE.

I look at nature, and I see how much it is thriving. I look at animals, plants, and life blooming with success. All things in nature are sustained and provided for. I am going to notice the abundance the universe already provides, and stay in that frequency. Abundance surrounds me. I was born naturally abundant.

52. I AM SO GRATEFUL FOR ALL THE MONEY I HAVE.

I am grateful for all the money I have in my account right now. I bless it, and know that it is growing every day.

53. I LIVE IN COMFORT AND JOY.

I have no worries. I have no concerns. I have everything I need. Whatever I want to buy, I buy. I focus on enjoying my life experiences and doing what I love. The feeling I have right now of living it up is attracting so much abundance into my life.

54. I TRAVEL THE WORLD.

The earth is my playground. I get to go see different countries, learn about different cultures, and connect with different people. The universe provides ways for me to have the best experiences out of life, because I want it and deserve it.

55. I VISUALIZE A CONSTANT FLOW OF MONEY.

In my mind, I see a constant flow of money entering my life. It is coming from all directions at a high rate of speed.

56. I ATTRACT SUCCESSFUL PEOPLE INTO MY LIFE.

I attract other successful people into my life who teach me what I need to know and connect me with greater opportunities. Successful people surround me.

57. I GET VISIONS OF IDEAS THAT PROVIDE ME WITH FINANCIAL FREEDOM.

The universe keeps giving me creative ideas and the energy to execute them. My next idea will give me the financial freedom I have been waiting for. A breakthrough is coming.

58. I SUPPORT THE PEOPLE I LOVE AND CARE ABOUT FINANCIALLY.

I see myself giving my family money out of the blue. They are all so excited, happy, and proud of me for making it. I am successful, and give money away easily and effortlessly. I am in the flow.

59. I DO WHAT I LOVE AND GET PAID FOR IT.

I do what I love, and I get paid for it. I don't even feel like I am working when I am doing what I am passionate about. Life is so good for me right now. I am so happy being free.

60. I MAKE ENOUGH MONEY TO HAVE FREE TIME AND EXPLORE LIFE.

I have financial security and freedom of time. I explore life. I learn new things. I eat new food. I travel to new places. With all the money I am making, I am also enriching my life with new experiences and lifelong memories.

61. THERE'S ENOUGH FOR EVERYONE.

Abundance surrounds me. Abundance surrounds everyone. There's more than enough. The more I believe this, the more I receive it. I am in the flow.

62. EVERY DAY, I INVEST IN MYSELF.

I get better so I can attract better. I do something every day that adds to my financial success. My energy is productive and lucrative. I put out and receive back in large quantities.

63. I READ, STUDY, AND LEARN ABOUT WEALTH CREATION.

I read books that teach me about business. I study other successful people. I expand my mind daily and increase my awareness. The more I learn, the more I can do. I can see the bigger picture, and I can execute it.

64. I AM LIVING MY DREAMS.

My visions have manifested. I am living in my dream home. I have bought my dream car. I am in the flow, and it feels so good.

65. I HELP THOSE IN NEED.

I do unexpected good. I keep the flow going. I keep the blessings going.

66. I RELEASE ANY RESISTANCE I HAVE TO MONEY.

I release, let go, and remove any resistance, fears, or beliefs I have about money. Having money is a good thing. I welcome it into my life. I enjoy it. I spend it freely.

67. I AM IN THE MOOD TO RECEIVE MONEY OUT OF NOWHERE.

I love getting unexpected money out of the blue.

I TRUST That the Universe Will Provide for Me Affirmations

"And, when you want something, all the universe conspires in helping you to achieve it." — Paul Coelho

The next set of affirmations will keep your faith up as you wait for your planted vision to come to fruition. These are strong words that will help you during the manifestation process so you can trust and believe in yourself even more.

68. I AM NOT GOING TO WORRY ABOUT HOW THINGS WILL HAPPEN.

I am not going to worry about how things will happen; I will simply believe that they will happen for me. Great things are aligning for me because I put that energy out, and now it is all manifesting perfectly. I trust it. I believe it.

69. I TRUST IN DIVINE TIMING.

Once I set my intentions and put my vision out for what I want to manifest, I'll just relax and let the universe do its work. I will be in an expectant state of good news.

70. MY VISION IS MANIFESTING.

My thoughts are so powerful that when I send them out, they are already working and aligning everything for me. Paths are being opened. Roads are being cleared. My vision is making its way toward me. It's arriving right away. I feel it here already.

71. BEING PATIENT IS SO IMPORTANT.

The most powerful thing I can do right now is be patient. I know everything I want to manifest in my life will happen for me when I remain patient and trust the process.

72. I TRUST THE UNIVERSE.

I trust the universe to bring me everything I need in the right time, context, and order.

73. I BELIEVE IN THE UNSEEN.

I believe it in order to see it. Everything starts in the mind first. The visions I have will manifest.

74. TODAY, I CHOOSE TO BELIEVE EVEN MORE.

The days doubt tries to come in, I choose to believe even more. I refuse to allow my past thinking to block my blessings. I trust with all my heart. I believe with all my might. I will not get in the way of my blessings. I will charge my manifesting energy with the power of unwavering faith today. I got this.

75. I BELIEVE IN MYSELF.

Today, I choose to remember how many blessings have manifested in my life. The days I thought I couldn't make it, I did. The times I thought I was in need of something, I got it. The universe has never failed me before, and it won't in the future—ever. I just have to keep believing in myself.

76. WHAT BELONGS IN MY LIFE IS ON THE WAY RIGHT NOW.

What belongs to me will effortlessly flow into my life. Instead of worrying about how it will happen, I'll just relax and be in a deserving state to receive. I believe that it is already mine. I own the energy of what I want to receive by being it.

77. ALL THINGS START ON THE MENTAL PLANE FIRST.

Everything happens on the mental level before it manifests into the physical. This is why it's so important for me to remember that what I am manifesting is on the way. I trust that. I have to keep believing, no matter what the external circumstances or environment. I choose to strengthen my vision and have hope that things can get better.

78. I GOT THIS.

Even when things get uncomfortable, I still have the attitude of *I got this!* Everything that is happening to me is only upgrading me and preparing me for what's about to come into my life. I can't be scared or avoid it. I have to welcome new energy. I have to be prepared to match the frequency of the energy I am trying to manifest.

79. I LET GO AND MAKE ROOM FOR NEW ENERGY.

I have decided to start eliminating things that don't add positivity, love, and hope into my life. I am making these changes to make room for the arrival of something greater. I can't hold onto things and expect better. I have to clear the way and open the portals for a new frequency to flow into my life.

80. GOOD NEWS IS COMING.

Great news is on the way. I believe it. I feel it.

I AM GRATEFUL for All I Have Manifested Affirmations

"Gratitude opens the door to the power, the wisdom, the creativity of the universe." — Deepak Chopra

The next set of affirmations will help you be in a grateful energy state so you can start to receive more. If you never notice the blessings surrounding you, you'll only be missing out on how much the universe has already given you. Gratitude is a powerful energy that speeds up your ability to manifest.

81. BLESSINGS ARE FLOODING IN.

I am counting my blessings every day, and I notice more blessings entering my life. Today, I am just so grateful to be alive and breathing.

82. I HAVE EVERYTHING I NEED.

I have manifested everything I have asked for. Thank you, universe, for constantly aligning me with my greatest visions and helping me manifest my wildest dreams. I am forever grateful.

83. I WALK, TALK, AND SPEAK GRATITUDE.

Once I set my intentions, I start to speak as if they have already happened. I start to walk around and count my blessings. I start to speak and say what I am grateful for. I feel the energy shift inside me.

84. I AM GRATEFUL FOR EVERYTHING I HAVE.

I am so grateful for everything I have. I am grateful for my health, wellness, mindset, abundance, family, friends, love, and inner peace. I have everything I need to do greater things for the world. Thank you, universe. I am blessed.

85. EVERY DAY, I AM GRATEFUL.

Every morning, I count my blessings and speak what I want to experience for that day. I know how powerful my energy is, and I am going to use it to create more things to be grateful for in my life.

86. I INVITE GRATITUDE INTO MY HEART.

I am filled with so much gratitude that it pours out of me to share with others. I am grateful for the simple things. When I notice the blessings the universe has already provided for me, I get more excited and happy to share them with the world.

Affirmations to Optimize Your Physical Body

"Take good care of your body. It's the only place you have to live." — Jim Rohn

The next set of affirmations will give you the energy to mentally empower yourself to make physical changes that help you have more energy and feel good about yourself. To change the body, the mind must first be shifted. Use these affirmations to help you move in the direction of your desired outcome.

87. I HAVE A LOT OF ENERGY.

I have a lot of energy to do creative work, complete my vision, and create my ideas. The universe supplies me with endless energy to do the best I can. I can feel a rush of energy all over my body. I receive high energy daily.

88. I EAT HIGHLY NUTRITIOUS FOODS.

I take good care of my body. I eat food that is high in nutrients so I can be fit, healthy, and feel good about myself. I love my body. I give it the best food.

89. I WORK OUT.

I do some kind of workout every day. I move my body to keep my energy flowing. I feel healthy. I am happy with my changes and new way of living my life.

90. I LOVE MY BODY.

I love my body. I feel good in my body. I accept myself. I am making positive changes because I am starting to feel good about myself every day. All the results I want are happening when I constantly take it one day at a time. I got this.

91. I DO SELF-CARE TREATMENTS.

I do some kind of self-care treatment for my body, like a massage or spa visit, once a month at minimum. When I take care of myself, I feel good, and that's the frequency I am on every day.

92. I RADIATE POSITIVE ENERGY.

My aura and energy radiate health. I am surrounded by a powerful source of loving, peaceful, and supportive energy that gives even more life and energy. I feel so healthy. I feel so whole. I radiate so brightly. I shine.

93. MY BODY IS POWERFUL.

My body is so intelligent. My body knows how to heal itself. My body is always supporting me. I am going to be kinder, more loving, and more connected to my body.

I BELIEVE in Myself Affirmations

"We are what we believe we are." — *C. S. Lewis*

The next set of affirmations will help you believe in yourself and remember that you are a spirit having a physical experience. You will also become aware of the subtle energy that flows through you and empowers you. Once you continuously affirm this, you will discover how powerful you already are.

94. I AM A POWERFUL BEING.

I am beyond the physical. I am beyond any limitations. I am a spirit. I know that I am having a physical experience, but the energy that flows through me is beyond space and time. I will focus my mind on that energy to create a powerful vision for myself within my imagination. What I see will manifest. Everything starts with a thought.

95. I CAN HAVE ANYTHING; I CAN ATTRACT EVERYTHING.

The universe has no limitations. I am limitless. I can attract anything I want.

96. EVERYTHING IS ENERGY.

I have manifested so much in my life. When I look around me, I can tell that everything I have always wanted started off as a thought. When I had the thought and put energy into it, it manifested. I can do the same thing again and again. All I have to do now is notice that everything is energy forming into a physical existence, just like my spirit within my body.

97. I HAVE TO CONCENTRATE MY MENTAL ENERGY.

Now that I know the power of my thoughts, I am going to start focusing and concentrating my mental energy to manifest my vision. Every day, I will concentrate for 10 minutes on a single vision, and build from there.

98. I BELIEVE FIRST, AND SEE LATER.

I am a strong believer in my imagination. What I imagine will come to life. I don't let external reality distract me from my goal. I will remain unmoved and unbothered by external challenges. I believe in myself. I believe that it will happen for me. Nothing can stop me.

99. GREAT THINGS ARE COMING MY WAY.

Now that I have put my vision together and set my intentions, I will keep on believing in it until it comes into my reality. I will keep telling myself *GREAT THINGS ARE COMING MY WAY* every single day!

100. I AM SO BLESSED TO RECEIVE THIS CLARITY AND INSIGHT.

I am so blessed to receive these affirmations and words that I will be using to manifest what I want. I will repeat, speak, think, and feel these words so I can stay energized, uplifted, and inspired to create my reality.

Now that you have these 100 powerful affirmations at your disposal, you can repeat them daily, and use them as a tool to help yourself stay focused during the manifestation process. You can even add some of your own by starting each one with "I am...." Give yourself permission to dream and let go. Allow yourself to feel all of these words, and believe them until they become part of your thought patterns. Be patient with yourself, as you are reprogramming your mindset to one of abundance, happiness, love, and complete freedom. There is nothing stopping you from having it all. Believe in yourself. You got this!

15

Magnetic Money Mindset

Feel Abundant and Live Financially Free

*I am prosperous, wealthy,
and living my best life.*

Welcome to the magnetic money mindset section of this book. So many people have asked me questions about how they can make more money or manifest financial freedom. When I get these questions, I have always realized that the people asking have forgotten that they are the powerful source that creates wealth. How someone feels about money determines how much of it he or she attracts. Some people want money, but they feel like they are not worthy or deserving of it, because they put too much value on the dollar amount and not on themselves. Without the human concepts assigned to it, money would just be a piece of paper.

The point of this section is to remember that you are the creative mind that attracts, creates, and moves money around. You are the creative mind that produces value for other people. What are you offering the world? Do you feel good when you see other successful people, or do you feel resentment/hate? This section will teach you how to identify and remove the thought patterns that are limiting you from having the financial freedom you deserve. You will also learn how to tap into your creative abilities to generate ideas, businesses, and value for the world.

Another important lesson you'll learn is realizing that your mindset and how you see the world are what create your experiences and what you do.

You can activate the magnetic money mindset right now, and start to attract financial freedom. If you want to get your business started and make it profitable, you'll find a visualization technique below. If you already have customers and clients and want to secure more, this section will help you with that, as well.

You will need to learn the art of feeling worthy and deserving of receiving money. One thing you should never forget is that you are the value. The minute you act like something outside of you is more worthy, or put material things on a pedestal instead of yourself as the creator and attractor of all things, you fail to realize who you really are. Manifesting success is feeling successful and worthy already. A lot of people have forgotten that they are already abundant, and that money surrounds them daily.

The goal is to shift your mindset from scarcity to abundance. The opportunities and blessings are in your hands right now. You can be financially free, and live a comfortable life in which you'll no longer be worrying about just surviving. Instead, you'll be actually living life.

You don't have to live paycheck to paycheck. You don't have to be limited. You are deserving of the experiences you want. My goal is to help you shift your current mindset to the magnetic money mindset, so each thought you have and each action you take results in financial freedom. Be ready to manifest unlimited sources of abundance and attract great opportunities that will help you in the process of living the life you have always wanted.

You Are a Creative Being

The first thing you need to understand is that all things come from the mind. You are a creative being, connected to the universal source that provides for all. If you look around you, you'll see the creativity of the human mind. Everything that surrounds you was once someone's idea or thought. Take this in before you even get into the steps of manifesting money. Recognize the genius within you and all humans. Our mindset is the most important thing that either attracts abundance to us or repels it. There is no difference between you and someone who is extremely successful and wealthy. The only thing they did differently was to connect with the unlimited source, which provided them with ideas—and they followed through. They took action.

This is the biggest problem faced by people who don't already have what they want. Ideas are unlimited, but action and execution are rare. How many times have you gotten profound ideas for creating a product, business, or service? Did you just ponder the thought, or did you take action to get it done? Did fear stop you from living your dream and getting out of your comfort zone? Do you self-sabotage by thinking you can't do it? This wisdom is for you...to realize that you are limitless. You have access to many ideas that can help people. You, too, can be part of the marketplace and join the economy of creating businesses that serve and bring value to the world.

Understand that now, more than ever in the history of humanity, there are so many opportunities to make money. The Internet has connected people from all over the world, and ideas, services, and businesses are thriving. There is no shortage of abundance; there are only people who haven't joined the market to share their creative ideas.

The more you feel good about money and living life abundantly, the more money you will attract. If you believe that you can have more, the universe will present you more opportunities to receive. Don't worry about how it will happen. Just keep on believing that you deserve financial freedom, and that you will follow through with any and all action necessary on your end to make it happen.

In the next pages of this section, I will help you identify and remove any limiting belief systems about money, and teach you how to tap into your inner wealth and begin manifesting.

What Is Your Relationship with Money?

What you think and how you feel about money is what determines how much of it you get. A lot of people have been raised to believe that money is evil, or that money and spirituality don't mix. This type of mindset limits people from having what they want, because they think they are being too materialistic and physical. Money is neutral. What you think of it is what you get. This is why it is very important to identify the limiting beliefs you hold about it—so you can begin to remove any blocks or limitations that stand in your way.

Understand that your relationship with money stems from how you were raised and what your family thought about money. Were you constantly feeling lack? Did your parents always tell you, "We can't afford that?" Was money attached to hard work and sacrifice instead of creativity and freedom? Were you taught about finances? All of these things can be the cause of how much money you make, and what you think and feel about money.

Take a moment to write down the beliefs you have about money. You have to be honest with yourself, so you can remove any limitations or blocks that stand in the way of your magnetic money mindset. Everything is about shifting how you think to more abundance and freedom. If you think you can receive something, then you will. This is a good time to take out a piece of paper and answer the following questions:

What do you think about money?

Is money good or evil?

Do you feel good or bad about spending money?

How do people who have a lot of money make you feel?

Are you happy for others who have success, or are you resentful?

Do you believe that financial freedom requires physical work?

Are you a creative person?

Do you get million-dollar ideas?

Do you take action when you get million-dollar ideas?

Do you believe you'll be financially free?

Do you read books on business?

Do you study others who are successful?

Do you feel like there's enough money for everyone to succeed?

These questions might trigger feelings within you, and the predominant thoughts that come up can be the beliefs you have about money. Nothing is limiting you right now from having what you want. You have to start switching your mindset to one of abundance, creativity, fun, and living financially free.

How to Remove Limiting Beliefs About Money

First things first. You have to understand that there is an abundance of money going around at any given time. The only thing stopping you from having your share of the abundance is your mindset. Limiting beliefs about money could include the idea that it is hard to get, or that there isn't enough to go around. Some people have a negative view of rich people, and think that the rich are getting richer and the poor are getting poorer. Anytime there is external blame, you block yourself from the universal source that is all-giving and all-providing for those who believe and are ready to receive. Once you start to understand that your limiting beliefs are taught and not a natural part of your soul, you'll begin to free yourself from what holds you down.

You have to tell yourself that you believe in yourself. You also have to feel good about having money, and believe that you can have more. Removing limiting beliefs means getting rid of the thought patterns that hold you back from having abundance. You must be happy for people who have money and have succeeded. Feeling good and happy for others is a good way to attract the same blessings to yourself. What is your usual conversation about money? Do you always complain that you don't have enough, or do you believe that money is coming your way? When you give your energy and attention to limiting beliefs, you block blessings and opportunities from entering your life. This is a good time to start being conscious about what you feel and say when it comes to being financially free.

Are you doing what you love? Do you have a passion? So many people have jobs they hate, because they are afraid to follow their dreams. Doing something you don't like lowers your vibration and makes you feel badly about yourself and your contribution to the world. Never do anything that makes you feel badly about yourself, or anything that depletes your energy. Some of the most successful people in the world have taken risks to challenge their fears and overcome their limiting beliefs. Many have given up jobs they hated to follow their passion. Is what you are doing with your life right now making you feel good, or is it making you feel low in energy?

You have to learn and discover what your passions are, so you can bring value to the world with your ideas and creativity. There is enough money for everyone to be financially free. How can you provide value to people? What services can you offer? What can you teach others? There is something within you that knows you are meant to do more for the world. You have to follow your passion and take the risk of letting go of what doesn't serve your life goals. Be sure to have a strategic exit plan if you are planning to follow your dreams. Ask for guidance from the universe to help make your path and purpose clear. The answers you need and the opportunities you deserve will align to you.

Starting today, it is time for you to face your fears and remove what is stopping you from being financially free. Start with your mindset; replace negative, fearful thoughts with hopeful ones. Believe that you can manifest money.

To help you with the process of removing any limiting thoughts and feelings, I am going to ask you to do something for the next seven days. This will be an experiment you can incorporate into the Manifest Now technique we previously discussed.

You will have access to the universal bank, which gives you one million dollars per day to spend. At the end of the day, that million dollars will need to be completely used up, because you cannot take it into the next day. Each day, you will be given one million dollars to spend completely. This experiment will help you raise your frequency so you can feel good about money, but at the same time, it will make you step into the vision.

Each day, take out a journal and write down in detail exactly what you would do with a million dollars if you had it right now. Don't think about anything else but spending it and enjoying your life. What would be your first purchase? Be sure to spend this universal million dollars as if it were in your bank account right now. Let Google be your friend when it comes to searching prices of the things you would want. Next to each purchase, put the total amount. By the end of the day, you should have spent a million dollars. Realize that you can donate to charities, too, and give back. You can clear your debt, or help anyone you want. If you had a million dollars a day for the next seven days, what would you be doing? Be sure to keep track of the numbers and exactly what it is you're using the money for.

This is a powerful magnetic money mindset shifter. You will notice yourself feeling more relaxed and excited about your manifestations. Your energy will shift from limitation to abundance. You will notice that you can buy and have anything you want. Your mindset will start to be exposed to the feeling of having it all. You will feel abundant, wealthy, and extremely rich. You will also notice how small some of the problems you think you have really are. Get ready to set your frequency so high with this technique, and watch how many opportunities and ideas begin to find you.

Have a Business Already?

Here's How to Attract More Customers and Clients

If you already have a business and want to expand it and bring in more clients, then you need to start using the power of your mind and the Law of Attraction. Start visualizing more people being interested in your business and ideas. Feel the energy of large groups of people reaching out to you or contacting you for your services. Everything starts in the mind. Feel good that your business is growing and thriving. Don't focus on your reality right now. You probably created the results you have now with limiting thought patterns. Don't get hung up on what has already been created. It's fun and exciting to see that you can create a whole new reality at any time. Your income, the people you attract, and the opportunities you align with can completely change right now. Believe in that.

Create a visual experience of watching your income grow. See the numbers in your bank account growing daily. How does that feel for you? See yourself smiling and feeling good that you are financially free. How does *that* feel for you? Always power your visualization with positive emotions of excitement. There are billions of humans in the world. So many people are finding out about your business and wanting your services.

Another great way to grow your business is to take care of the clients and customers you already have. Treat them very well, and make sure to give positive energy to what you already have. This is a good way to show appreciation to the universe, and to demonstrate that you are thankful for all the blessings you are receiving.

Once you begin this magnetic money-mindset shift and increase your frequency, you will see yourself attracting more opportunities—and way more money. Everything is about what you think and feel. Always be in a state of gratitude. Believe that you can solve anything with the guidance of the unlimited universal supply. You can tap into the universal bank, and believe that everything you want to manifest is on the way.

Don't Be Afraid to Ask for Money and Increase Your Prices

One thing that stops many people from getting the money they deserve is that they are afraid to ask for it. They give away free services, and lowball themselves because they think if they charge less, more people will come. That is not the case. People with their own businesses create their own pricing. If someone feels good about what they are offering and they are good at it, they should understand that their value is priceless and charge more. Don't assume people can't afford it. This is a negative, limiting thought which says that people can't afford to pay for things. If this is the energy you're putting out, how can you create financial freedom? You have to switch your mindset to knowing your value and understanding what you deserve. If you're an expert at something and you offer great services, don't lowball yourself. The universe will always align you with people who want to spend money with you. How many luxury brands exist? They aren't worried about who can afford them or not. They just focus on creating value, and put it into the market for those who want to make the investment. It's always about providing value and something worth paying for.

Remember, when people deal with cheap products and services, they don't value them as highly. When they make an investment, they are more committed and dedicated to the service and business.

Get your energy in check, and know that you can charge based upon the value you offer. Ask for the money. Don't ever feel badly for asking for money for your services. You have a magnetic money mindset that pulls toward you clients who want to pay you, because you (and they) believe in what you are selling.

Money Buys You Experiences

What do you want to experience in this life? What do you consider comfortable living? What would having everything you want consist of? Remember that when your energy is focused on an experience you want, money manifests more quickly. Most people who want money don't really know what they would do with it. You need to have an exact understanding of what you would do if you had financial freedom right now. This is why I did the one-million-dollars-a-day experiment above—so you could get clear about what you want out of life.

What is your dream? It's not about hoarding money in your bank and being scared of spending it. What do you want from this life? How do you want to enjoy yourself? What are your standards of living a quality life? Who do you want to help? How would you give back? All of these questions are here for you to think about and feel. Connect with the experiences you want out of life. Make a clear plan for what you want to manifest.

In the next ten days, what do you want to manifest?

In the next month?

In the next two months?

In the next year?

Have the energy of knowing that the things you want to manifest are already here and on their way. Begin to check off each of your manifestations, and celebrate them. Money is here to buy you experiences and take you all over the world, if that is something you want to do. Money gives you freedom to do whatever you want. When you spend money, think of the people you are helping and supporting. Keep the circulation going, and know that plenty more is coming your way. The goal here is for you to know what you want to do with money when you have it. Invest in living it up and enjoying life.

Those Who Feel Abundant Always Attract Abundance

From this day on, feel good about money. Feel good about what is already in your bank account. Bless every dollar you spend, and know that it will return to you tenfold. You never have to stress or worry anymore about how you will pay for things or get opportunities. You have to start maintaining a wealthy mindset, and understand that you have access to the unlimited source of abundance, which can implant a powerful idea in your mind right now. When you are happy and grateful, you are more creative. Allow yourself to flow, and trust the universe. Money is coming to you in large quantities because you feel good and deserve it. You spend freely because you have plenty. Create a gratitude journal for all the blessings you have and all the things you are about to manifest. Show the universe that you feel deserving and worthy because you are already happy and thankful for the resources and opportunities you have—and the ones that keep coming your way. Stay in an expectant spirit and energy that something incredible is about to happen for you. You are very rich, and the magnetic money mindset is pulling wealth toward you at every moment. Be on the lookout for large sums of money, and the many opportunities that are coming your way to do and create what you want. The universe is about to bless you financially.

16

Start Manifesting Now -
All Things Are Possible

Now that you have learned how to manifest and create the best reality for yourself, it is time to get started on the manifestation process. What you will receive by applying this wisdom is endless. It is up to you to be a conscious creator and speak what you want into existence. There is no more doubting, overthinking, worrying, or blocking your own blessings. You deserve everything you are about to receive because you believe in yourself. You are a magnetic manifestor. You pull into your life the energy that matches your inner state. You are a high-frequency being creating the life you want. Happiness, abundance, love, and joy are in your hands. You are already surrounded by everything you want. Shift your mindset so you can see it. Feel it within your emotions so it is already real for you.

After you have done your part and told the universe what you want to manifest, watch for signs, synchronizations, and alignments. The universe will get to work for you right away. The universe will bend to your favor and start helping you manifest. When opportunities show up, take them. When you get signs, follow them. You might attract people, new awareness, and ideas. You will even be put in situations that will help you manifest what you want. Be open to miracles and unexpected blessings. The universe does work in mysterious ways, so be open to more than what you're used to. Keep the balance between visualizing, creating, and taking action, while at the same time flowing, allowing, and trusting the process.

Once you manifest what you want, nothing can ever stop you from believing that you create your reality. A powerful feeling will come over you which you'll recognize as your spirit reminding you of your inner potential. When you know what you can do, share it with the world. Tell people about this power and the miracles that can happen for them. Let your results inspire others. Share this book with your family and friends so they, too, can discover what they have access to. Keep applying the wisdom, tools, and techniques offered in this book. Keep allowing yourself to be guided to further expand and reach your highest ideals. There are unlimited possibilities waiting for you to manifest. Go out there and manifest your wildest dreams. I believe in you.

CPSIA information can be obtained
at www.ICGtesting.com
Printed in the USA
BVHW030255160820
586548BV00003B/305